Dianne II
Cook & Tell

BY DIANNE CAGE

Cover by John Derryberry

Pen & Ink Drawings by
Lori Young

Garden District Books, 2005

I said never, he said "You really should!"

This one is for you, my biggest fan and partner,

MIKE CAGE

and all our children:
SATCHIE, GEORGE, JANELLE, SALLIE,
LAURA, JESSE, MARY, AMANDA,
KATHERINE. HANNAH, SARA, LESSLEY,
VIRGINIA, THOMAS, LIZ, WALTER, JOHN,
CLAIRE, MIKE, MICHELE, TAYLOR,
JORDAN, and of course, ROLEX.

TABLE OF CONTENTS

INTRODUCTION

Cooking & Gardening with Dianne was my first book and I'll be refer-
ring to it for recipes and cross references, as *Cooking & Gardening*.

GARDENING PLEASURES

Enjoy some gardening tips and ideas that my husband and I have fun
with and love in our beautiful garden. We are in zone 8 which is based
on the map of the United States Department of Agriculture. Enjoy and
be creative with your garden.

REMEMBERING MAMA!

Enjoy short stories and fun sayings that I have collected over the years!

THE ART OF LIVING WELL

"You only live once, but if you do it right, once is enough." *~Joe Lewis*

As they say, if you have never made a mistake, you have never done
anything. To live a good happy life we have to have our higher power,
our GOD, and good health. Your body is your temple. Someone said,
"if I had known I was going to live this long, I would have taken better
care of myself." You are what you eat! Let's eat right, exercise, be kind
and treat others as you want to be treated and have fun! EVERTHING
IN MODERATION! WISE CHOICES AND PORTION CONTROL!

Food is the art of table, the art of the plate. Food evokes memories
and is an individual reflection of our past. To some people a recipe
is not just a piece of paper but a piece of their soul, piece of their
self-esteem, piece of their pride and a place in a family. I have tried
to give credit where credit is due and it is really hard. When a recipe
in question is in many different books and magazines, whose was it,
whose is it? A recipe is style, your style; you put your touch, flair and
swing into it. It is yours. Food and entertaining is a reflection of one's
graciousness, the precision of taste in food, flowers, decor and mood.
When entertaining, in small groups, try and have people that have
common interests, something they all enjoy. Pay special attention to
special likes and dislikes of your guests. Who you have is very important. One thing for sure, if you are happy, relaxed and having fun,
your guests will depart with a smile on their face and look forward to
the next time.

ENJOY & JOIE DE VIVE!

Dianne

Party

Foods

CRABMEAT MARINATED

FRESH, JUMBO LUMP! You want to do something really extra special AND so wonderful...THIS IS IT!!! This is for a large cocktail party. I make this when crab season is at its peak!

1   **onion, coarsely chopped**
2   **Tablespoons sugar**
4   **pounds jumbo lump crabmeat**
1   **cup finely chopped parsley**
1½ **cups finely chopped green onions – Tops and bottoms**
1   **cup small capers**
½   **cup olive oil**
½   **cup cider vinegar**
½   **cup lemon juice**
2-3 **Tablespoons lemon zest**
   Salt, pepper and Old Bay seasoning to taste
1   **cup mayonnaise**
½   **cup prepared mustard**
   Toast points
   Garnish: Chopped parsley

Cover onions with cold water. Add sugar. Refrigerate 1 hour or overnight. Drain well. Very carefully so as not to break up the lumps, drain the crabmeat and check for shells. Gently toss in parsley, onions and capers. Whisk rest of ingredients and pour over crabmeat mixture. Place in a Tupper Ware container, cover very tightly and refrigerate until ready to serve. Several times before serving, turn over quickly so marinate can cover all crabmeat.

Serve in a big pretty crystal bowl with homemade toast points. Garnish with fresh parsley.

When using fresh crabmeat, always, very gently, check for shells.

CRABMEAT MORNAY

1	stick butter
1	bunch green onions, minced
1	bunch parsley, minced
2	Tablespoons all-purpose flour
1	pint heavy cream or fat free half-and-half
1	8-ounce package shredded Swiss cheese
2	Tablespoons dry sherry
	Cayenne pepper and salt to taste
½	cup capers
2	pounds lump crabmeat
	Melba rounds

Melt butter in a heavy stock-pot. Saute onions and parsley. Whisk in flour until bubbly. Add cream and cheese. Stir until well blended. Add sherry, cayenne, salt and capers. Fold in crabmeat. Serve in chafing dish with Melba rounds.

Pretty for a lunch patty shells with a green salad and a pickled peach.

OYSTERS MOSCA

So easy and a crowd pleaser! Perfect for a big Cocktail party! Have 6 or so big Pyrex dishes that fit into silver or copper holders and replace oysters as needed! Serve with toothpicks. This is, also, a perfect appetizer!

2	cups seasoned breadcrumbs
1	Tablespoon crushed red pepper
	Juice of 2 lemons
1	Tablespoon finely grated lemon zest
¾	cup olive oil
1-2	garlic cloves, crushed
3	Tablespoons chopped parsley
1	cup Parmesan cheese
	Salt to taste
2	pounds large oysters, rinsed and drained
	Garnish: Paprika

Combine all ingredients except oysters. Place oysters in a baking dish, ramekins or shells. Top with mixture and sprinkle with paprika. Bake at 350 degrees until oysters curl.

Oysters are the best in the "R" Months, when the waters are good and cold!

DEVILED OYSTERS

Outstanding for your big cocktail parties, perfect for a starter or a spectacular side dish with fresh grilled fish or a good steak. My friend SUZANNE WOLFF and I were always assigned to do this for the big parties around town.

Yield: 8-10 servings

1 stick butter
1 cup finely chopped parsley
1 cup chopped green onions, tops and bottoms
1 cup finely chopped bell pepper
2-3 garlic cloves, finely minced
3-4 dozen oysters, drained and coarsely chopped, save some juice
2 cups finely rolled cracker crumbs
Oyster juice
2 Tablespoons Worcestershire sauce
1 Tablespoon salt
1 teaspoon pepper
1 teaspoon cayenne pepper
¼ teaspoon dried thyme
Zest of 1 lemon
Juice of 1 lemon
2 large eggs, beaten
Garnish: Paprika
Toast points or Melba rounds

In a large pot, melt butter and sauté all the vegetables until tender. Add oysters and mix well. Soak cracker crumbs in about ½ cup oyster juice and add to mixture. Add seasonings. Fold in eggs and check seasonings. You want this spicy, with a nice lemony essence. Never have one seasoning over power the other, each should compliment the other. If something is missing, it is usually salt!

Sprinkle with a good Hungarian Paprika and serve. Can be served in ramekins, a big Pyrex dish or your chafing dish. Party toast points are perfect for this. If you do not have time to make the toast points, Melba rounds are a good substitute.

This freezes well, but never leave anything in the freezer too long! Except maybe pecans.

SHRIMP DIP

MAMA always made this one for our coke parties!
Come on now, you know, COCA-COLA parties in the 50's!

1   **8-ounce package cream cheese, softened**
1   **3-ounce package cream cheese, softened**
1   **cup mayonnaise**
1   **cup sour cream**
    Zest of 1 lemon
2   **Tablespoons lemon juice**
2   **4¼-ounce cans shrimp, drained**
1   **cup finely chopped celery**
1   **Tablespoon grated onion**
¼   **cup finely chopped parsley**
½   **cup finely chopped green onions**
½   **teaspoon garlic salt**
½   **teaspoon lemon pepper**
    Worcestershire sauce to taste
2-3 **dashes Tabasco sauce**
    Cayenne pepper to taste
    Potato chips or fresh vegetables

Cream the first 4 ingredients well. Add remaining and mix well. Check seasonings. Serve with potato chips or fresh vegetables.

It's also nice to hollow cherry tomatoes and stuff with the dip. Makes a very pretty platter!

This makes a perfect spread for tea sandwiches!

The canned shrimp are a must for this dip!

ARTICHOKE PARMESAN

A CLASSIC!

3   14-ounce cans
      artichokes, drained
      and coarsely
      chopped
1   cup mayonnaise
1½ cups grated Parmesan
      cheese or blue
      cheese
      Zest of 2 lemons
      Juice of 2 lemons
      Cayenne pepper to
      taste
1   4-ounce can chopped
      green chilies,
      drained, optional
      Melba rounds

Combine artichokes, may-
onnaise, cheese, zest, juice,
cayenne and chilies. Pour
mixture into a 13 x 9 x 2-
inch baking dish. Bake at
350 degrees 20 minutes
until hot and bubbly. Serve
with Melba rounds.

May serve at room temperature or as a side dish with
steak or chicken. Just top
with a sprinkle of Italian
breadcrumbs.

FOIE GRAS, PAN SEARED

What's good from the goose? A gander at Foie Gras! Foie Gras calls for champagne and good company to share it with. As fancy as it is, it comes from humble beginnings: it is simply the liver of the goose and the duck. The ancient Greeks, Egyptians and Romans enjoyed this delicacy.

A perfect appetizer for an elegant dinner party!

4	**2-ounce slices of fresh foie gras**
1	**pound fresh spinach**
2	**Tablespoons green onions, finely chopped**
¾	**cup port wine**
1	**Tablespoon balsamic vinegar**
	Salt and fresh cracked pepper to taste

Heat heavy skillet to high heat. Season foie gras with salt and pepper. Sear about 1½ to 2 minutes on each side. Remove to a warm plate and drain off most of the rendering.

In the same skillet, add onions and spinach and cook until soft. Add vinegar and wine, check seasonings. To serve, place spinach on each plate and top with a slice of foie gras. Pour a little sauce over it and serve.

COCKTAIL FILET OF BEEF

Passed in a crispy, buttery, garlic French loaf.

1   **large loaf French bread**
1   **stick butter**
2   **cloves garlic, cracked**
½   **cup dry parsley**
6   **or 8 pounds beef tenderloin of beef**
  Kitchen Bouquet
  Worchestershire sauce
  Olive oil
  Lemon juice and zest
  Lemon pepper
  Salt and pepper
  Fresh parsley for garnish

Slice top of bread lengthwise and hollow out. Melt butter, garlic and parsley and brush inside bread and top. Toast in a 300 degree oven about 25 minutes.

Meanwhile, rub the beef with Kitchen Bouquet and marinate in the rest of the ingredients. An hour or so before serving, cook beef on the grill or in a hot oven or quick in a hot skillet. Be sure that you do not overcook. The meat should be more on the rare side.

When ready to serve, cut in bite-sized pieces. Serve with toothpicks in the French bread, placed on a big serving tray. Decorate with lots of fresh parsley. Pass with a good creamy horseradish sauce.

PULL BREAD: When hollowing out the French bread, use a fork and sharp knife. Try to get rather large pieces of the bread. Brush each piece with the butter, garlic and parsley mixture. When ready to serve, toast in a 300 degree oven for about 20 to 25 minutes and serve with your favorite soup or meal!

HOGSHEAD CHEESE (SOUSE)

The easy way! (I just wish it had a better name!) It's just not the Christmas Season without hogshead cheese! This is a perfect gift for a little holiday remembrance.

2 **head cheeses**
1 **small jar, green salad olives**
  Capers
  Seasonings to taste

At your favorite market or deli, pick out two head cheeses that you like. They will let you sample. Melt the cheeses down in a double boiler and cool slightly. Add chopped green salad olives and pimentos if you like. Pour mixture into Cuisinart and bump it two or three times.

I do not like big pieces of the meat or vegetables in my souse. You can add a few capers or extra seasonings if you like.

Pour the mixture into a pig mold, loaf pan, or it's really pretty poured into the styrofoam egg cartons or small muffin tins. The little individual bites are so pretty on a big platter and nice to pass at your holiday parties.

Serve with saltine crackers, a little hot pepper sauce and lemon wedges. Decorate your platter with lots of fresh parsley.

ESCARGOT

Snails and puppy dog tails! Different, pretty and good for a big cocktail party or reception.

1   lb. good quality sweet
      butter
5-6 pods, fresh garlic,
      finely minced
1   gallon, large snails,
      drained
1½ cups parsley, finely
      chopped
      Salt, pepper, and red
      pepper to taste

Melt butter in a large pot, add garlic, snails and sauté for about five minutes. Add parsley and seasonings. Simmer slowly for about 15 minutes. Serve warm in a big silver chafing dish. Serve with homemade toast points.

BAKED VIDALIA ONION DIP

2   Tablespoons butter
3   large Vidalia onions,
      coarsely chopped
2   cups shredded Swiss
      cheese
2   cups mayonnaise
1   8-ounce can sliced
      water chestnuts,
      drained and
      chopped
¼   cup white wine
2   garlic cloves, minced
1   teaspoon Tabasco
      sauce
      Cayenne pepper to
      taste
      Tortilla chips or
      crackers

Melt butter in a large skillet over medium high heat; add onion and sauté 10 minutes or until tender. Stir together cheese and next 5 ingredients; add to onion mixture, blending well. Spoon mixture into a lightly greased 2 quart baking dish. Bake at 375 degrees for 25 minutes and let stand 10 minutes. Serve with tortilla chips or crackers.

KICKING KRACKERS

4   sleeves premium
      crackers
1½ cups Canola oil
2   to 3 Tablespoons
      cracked red pepper
1   package dry ranch
      dressing

In a large Tupperware container, with a tight cover, add crackers. Whisk together oil, Pepper and Ranch dressing mix. Drizzle over crackers. Turn every 15 minutes for one hour. Store in airtight containers. These last indefinitely and are great with a little libation or a good salad. These also make nice little hostess gifts!

VIDALIA ONION DIP OR GARNISH

My friend PAT GODFREY made this at the beach and I thought it was fresh lump crabmeat! Sweet as sugar are these wonderful onions! Only make this dip with Vidalia Onions as they are very high in sugar content, and that is what makes it so good!

2   large Vidalia onions, medium to finely chopped
½   cup sugar
¾   cup rice wine vinegar
1   cup mayonnaise
2   Tablespoons lemon juice
½   cup finely chopped parsley
1   teaspoon Old Bay seasoning
½   teaspoon cayenne pepper
1   pound lump crabmeat, drained, optional
Garnish: Parsley and paprika
Toasted crackers

In a large bowl, marinate onions in sugar and vinegar. Cover and refrigerate over night. Drain and mix in all other ingredients. Check Seasonings. Garnish with fresh parsley and paprika. Serve with crackers.

If you use the crabmeat, mix and season dip to your taste and gently fold in crabmeat. This garnish is wonderful mixed in with a good fresh green salad.

PARTY HEARTY PARTY BALL

One of my favorite nephews, Dr. Charles Ebert Brown III, (Trey) whips this up in a New Orleans second. A perfect hor d'oeuvre with your afternoon libation. Really good, really easy and a great crowd pleaser! Since Miss Robin Seretta has entered the picture, I think Dr. Brown has moved up to a more elegant fare!

Yield: 8 servings

1 8-ounce package cream cheese, softened, may use fat free

1 2½-ounce jar dried beef, finely chopped

1 bunch green onions, finely chopped, tops and bottoms

1 4-ounce can pitted black olives, finely chopped

1 4-ounce can mushroom pieces, finely chopped

½ cups pecans, lightly toasted and finely chopped
    Garnish: Cayenne pepper and parsley
    Assorted crackers and fresh vegetables

Place cheese in a bowl and whip with a fork. Add next four ingredients and mix well. Place mixture in plastic wrap and form a ball and chill. When good and cold roll ball in pecans. Serve on a pretty plate or cheese board. Garnish with fresh parsley and serve with your favorite cracker or vegetable sticks.

This is also a very good tea sandwich spread!

PHYLLO, BRIE AND JELLY APPETIZERS

2   10-ounce boxes mini
      phyllo dough shells
1   wedge Brie cheese,
      cut into pieces
1   12-ounce jar favorite
      jelly
      Pecans or almonds,
      finely chopped

Place shells on a baking sheet. Place a small piece of brie in bottom with shells. Top with a small dollop of jelly and sprinkle a few nuts on top. Bake in a 350 degree oven about 8 minutes or until cheese starts to melt. Serve warm!

These little jewels are so good and so pretty and so easy!

CHEESE SOUFFLÉ SANDWICHES

4   sticks butter,
      softened
4   5-ounce jars Old
      English Cheese,
      room temperature
1   teaspoon Tabasco
      sauce
1   teaspoon onion
      powder
1½ teaspoons
      Worcestershire
      sauce
1   teaspoon beau monde
      seasoning
1½ teaspoons dried dill
2½ loaves thin sliced
      bread

Beat butter and cheese until fluffy. Add Tabasco, onion powder, Worcestershire sauce, seasoning and dill. Spread mixture on 3 bread slices and stack slices. Spread mixture on sides of bread. Cut into 4 to 6 pieces. Place pieces on a wax paper-lined baking sheet. Continue spreading remaining bread. Freeze bread pieces. Store pieces in plastic bags. When ready to use, place bread pieces on a baking sheet. Bake at 325 degrees until golden brown. If thawed, bake 10 to 15 minutes until edges are browned.

BRIE EN PHYLLO

JANELLE and GEORGE SNELLINGS (my children) like to serve this at wine tasting parties!

12 sheets phyllo pastry
2   sticks sweet butter, melted
5   pounds whole Brie cheese, not fully ripe

Butter baking sheet large enough to hold Brie. Layer 5 buttered pastry sheets on baking sheet. Set Brie on phyllo. Fold pastry over cheese. Cover top of cheese with six sheets of pastry, brushing butter on each layer. Tuck ends of pastry under cheese. Fold remaining pastry into a 1-inch wide strip. Brush with butter. Cut into leaf shapes. Place pastry leaves on top of wrapped cheese. Brush again with butter. Bake at 350 degrees 20-30 minutes or until golden brown. Let stand at least 30 minutes before serving.

Phyllo dough usually comes in a 1 pound package, containing 24 or more sheets. It is located in the freezer section. Allow phyllo to defrost in the refrigerator for at least 2 days. When ready to work with dough, be sure it is completely defrosted. Unwrap dough, unroll it and cover immediately with a damp towel. Let sit 15 minutes. Moist phyllo is easier to handle. Have a damp cloth handy to moisten if necessary.

CURRIED CHICKEN TEA SANDWICHES

½ cup flaked coconut
½ cup chopped almonds
1 8 ounce package
    cream cheese,
    softened
2 Tablespoons orange
    marmalade
1½ teaspoons curry
    powder
¼ teaspoon salt
¼ teaspoon pepper
2 cups diced cooked
    chicken
12 ½-inch thick rye,
    wheat, or white
    bread slices
3 Tablespoons diced
    green onions

Bake coconut and almonds in a shallow baking pan at 350 degrees, stirring occasionally, for 5 to 10 minutes or until toasted.

Stir together cream cheese and next 4 ingredients, gently stirring in chicken. Spread the mixture evenly on bread slices, trimming the crust. Cut each slice into 3 strips and sprinkle with coconut, almonds, and green onions.

PINEAPPLE HORSERADISH

This is Diana Gentry Breens PINEAPPLE WONDERFUL, I call it! So pretty to serve and a real crowd pleaser and oh, so easy! ENJOY!

1 **large pineapple, with a pretty top**
1 **8-ounce package cream cheese, softened**
1 **10-ounce jar pineapple preserves**
3 **Tablespoons horseradish**
1 **Tablespoon dry mustard**
   White tortilla chips

Cut the top of pineapple, up at the top and core pineapple, leaving the shell in tact. Have the pineapple for breakfast! Drain well. Mix remaining ingredients.. Pour mixture in pineapple shell, place on a big tray. Place the top of the pineapple by the filled shell. Spread chips all around to dip this wonderful mixture. Pretty on your table and an absolutely beautiful presentation and really wonderful! You may need to double this to refill your pineapple. because one recipe is not enough, it is so good.

Do not use fresh pineapple in a congealed jello salad. The papain in the pineapple will not let the jello congeal. I learned this the hard way!

BLACK BEAN, AVOCADO AND TOMATO SALSA

This is a MIKE CAGE favorite and is WONDERFUL! My daughter SATCHIE makes this best, don't know why but hers is really good.

The secret of this recipe is the fresh key lime juice!

Yield: 15-20 servings

2　16-ounce cans black beans, drained and rinsed
1　11-ounce can white shoepeg corn, drained and rinsed
2-3　Hess avocados, diced and sprinkled with lime juice
1½　cups diced tomatoes, drained
1　cup finely chopped green onions, tops and bottoms
1　cup finely chopped red onion or Vidalia onion
1　cup finely chopped jalapeño or serrano pepper
½　cup finely chopped bell pepper
¾　cup finely chopped cilantro
½　cup Key lime juice
¼　cup red wine vinegar
1½　teaspoons salt
1　teaspoon ground cumin
½　teaspoon chili powder
½　teaspoon garlic powder
　Tortilla chips

Mix all ingredients. Check seasonings, Chill and serve with fresh tostadas. You can add more peppers if you like. Always check your seasonings, if something is missing, it is usually salt, this recipe is easily halved.

Serve with the Tostitos with a hint of lime. A cup or so is really good tossed in with your green salad.

ENJOY!

I collect Hess avocados. I buy 6 or 8, really hard avocados, put them in a pretty wooden bowl, place them on my kitchen counter. In 2 or 3 days check to see if they are just soft and ripe. Place them in the refrigerator. They usually are fine for at least 2 weeks. You always have wonderful fresh avocado. Nothing makes a salad better than these butter sweet pears. They are good for you too!

CHILI HOT TAMALE FIESTA

Chile today, hot tamale...

This is wonderful for cocktail parties, served with tortilla chips! Perfect for a fun dinner party or supper club, served with a good green salad and tortilla chips. Pralines for dessert! PERFECT!!!

6	**to 8 hot tamales (from local Coney Island)**
1	**15-ounce can chili without beans**
½	**cup chopped peppers, of your choice**
1	**small onion, chopped**
1	**cup chopped green onions, tops and bottom**
1	**8-ounce package shredded sharp Cheddar cheese Tortilla chips**

Cut tamales in bite size pieces and place in a shallow baking dish. Cover with the chili and sprinkle with the peppers and half the onions. Cover with cheese, sprinkle with remaining onions and bake in a 350 degree oven for about 30 minutes or until hot and bubbly. Serve with chips.

Doubles or triples easily!

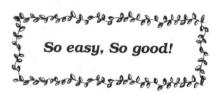

So easy, So good!

PICADILLO

This is a San Antonio "Fiesta Favorite!

1½ pounds ground beef
  or venison
1 bell pepper, chopped
1 onion, chopped
2-3 hot peppers, chopped
1 14½-ounce can
  chopped tomatoes
6 Tablespoons tomato
  paste
1 8-ounce can tomato
  sauce
½ teaspoon dried
  oregano
2 teaspoons ground
  cumin
1½ teaspoons cinnamon
½ teaspoon ground
  cloves
1 teaspoon sugar
½ cup sherry
½ cup dark raisins
½ cup golden raisins
  Salt, pepper and
  cayenne pepper to
  taste
1 cup toasted slivered
  almonds
  Tortilla chips

optional:
2 small potatoes,
  peeled and diced

Brown meat in a large stockpot. Drain well. Add bell peppers, onions, hot peppers, tomatoes, tomato paste, tomato sauce, oregano, cumin, cinnamon, cloves, sugar, sherry, all raisins, salt, pepper and cayenne. Simmer about 45 minutes. If mixture becomes too thick, add some water; or if too much liquid, drain.

This may be served on a chafing dish with corn chips, tortilla chips, or on warm flour tortillas. It is also good over rice. Garnish with minced green onions-tops and bottoms.

SOUTHWEST STYLE DRY ROASTED PECANS

This is a different swing for toasted pecans.

4   cups shelled pecans, rinsed
1   Tablespoon chili powder
1   Tablespoon ground cumin
1   Tablespoon cayenne pepper
1   to 2 Tablespoons salt
2   egg whites

In a big bowl, pour hot water over shelled pecans. Drain in a colander. Run really hot water over again. Check to make sure they are free of all shell and the little brown bitter stuff. Dry well in lots of paper towel. Beat egg whites really stiff. Add seasonings and mix well. Taste this mixture, it needs to be seasoned really strong. You may need to add more of all seasonings. Fold pecans into mixture, coating all well. Spread nuts out on a big baking sheet. Bake in a 300 degree over for about 1 hour, stirring every 15 minutes. The first 15 minutes, taste to see if the flavors are what you want. If needed sprinkle with more seasonings.

This is a different swing for toasted pecans! Kind of like BOOT SCOOTING PECANS!

PARTY PIMENTO CHEESE SPREAD

1   7-ounce can, diced pimentos
½ bottle Durkee's dressing
2   cups mayonnaise
2   Tablespoons lemon juice
1   teaspoon dry mustard
½ teaspoon Worcestershire sauce
½ teaspoon cayenne pepper
2   cloves, fresh garlic
2   lbs. sharp Cheddar cheese, grated
    Assorted crackers

In a food processor, add all ingredients except cheese and blend. Add cheese and beat until smooth. Chill and serve with toasted crackers or stuff in the tender stalk of celery!

OLIVE NUT SPREAD

6   ounces cream cheese, softened
½ cup mayonnaise
2   Tablespoons olive juice
    Dash of ground pepper
½ cup chopped pecans
1   cup chopped green olives

Combine the cream cheese and mayonnaise in a medium bowl and mix well. Add the olive juice and pepper to the mix. Gently fold in the pecans and green olives.

Serve these with your favorite crackers or perfect for sandwiches too.

PESTO, GOAT CHEESE AND SUN-DRIED TOMATO TART

1   cup loosely packed
     fresh basil
1   cup loosely packed
     fresh spinach
1½ teaspoons minced
     garlic
¼   cup olive oil
1   cup freshly grated
     Parmesan cheese
     Pepper to taste
1   8-ounce package
     cream cheese,
     softened
     4-ounces goat cheese,
     softened
½   cup sun-dried
     tomatoes packed
     in oil, drained and
     patted dry, minced
½   cup pine nuts,
     chopped
     Thinly sliced
     sun-dried tomatoes
     for garnish
     Assorted crackers or
     toast points

Chop basil, spinach and garlic in food processor. While machine is running, gradually add olive oil through the feeder tube. Add Parmesan and process until almost smooth. Season with pepper. Set aside. Blend cream cheese and goat cheese in a medium bowl until smooth.

Line a 3-cup bowl with plastic wrap, leaving a 4 inch overhang. Mold one third of cream cheese mixture into a disk shape and distribute evenly in bottom of prepared bowl. Spread half of basil mixture over cheese. Sprinkle with half sun-dried tomatoes, pine nuts and the last one third of cheese. Tap bowl lightly to allow ingredients to settle. Fold plastic overhang over top and refrigerate.

Thirty minutes before serving, unfold plastic wrap and invert onto serving plate. Decorate top with sun-dried tomato slices. Serve at room temperature with assorted gourmet crackers or homemade toast points.

This tart may be made several days ahead.

MUSHROOM BURGUNDY

4   sticks butter
1   quart hearty
    Burgundy
1   to 1½ Tablespoons
    Worcestershire
    sauce
1   teaspoon dried dill
1   teaspoon pepper
1   teaspoon garlic
    powder
2   cups boiling water
4   beef bouillon cubes
4   chicken bouillon
    cubes
4   pounds mushrooms,
    rinsed

Melt butter in a stockpot. Add Burgundy, Worcestershire sauce, dill, pepper, garlic, water, beef and chicken bouillon cubes. Stir in mushrooms. Bring to boil. Reduce heat, cover and simmer 3 to 5 hours. Remove cover and simmer additional 3 to 5 hours until liquid barely covers mushrooms. Cool to room temperature. Do not stir. Store in the refrigerator. Reheat to serve.

Mushrooms freeze well. This is an excellent accompaniment for grilled or roasted meats. This recipe doubles or triples easily and is perfect for a big party. Serve in a chafing dish or as a first course on toast points

PARTY TOAST

A must for really special occasions

1   16-ounce loaf thin
    sliced sandwich
    bread
1   stick butter
    Parsley to taste

Trim crust from bread. Melt butter and add parsley. Brush each bread slice with butter mixture. Cut into quarters. Arrange on a baking sheet. Bake at 225 degrees 40 minutes. Watch carefully. Toast should be crisp but not browned.

So elegant for dips!

STEAK TARTARE

5 pounds back strap or prime beef, grind before using
18 anchovy filets, well chopped
1½ onions, finely chopped
6 egg yolks
1 teaspoon salt
Pepper to taste
2 teaspoons Dijon mustard
1 teaspoon Tabasco sauce
½ cup small capers
⅓ cup minced chilies
¼ cup Cognac
Garnish: Parsley
Rye or pumpernickel

Combine beef, anchovies and onions. Mold into a mound. Make a well in center of the mixture. To well add egg yolks, salt, pepper, mustard, Tabasco, capers, chilies and Cognac. Mix well. Mold mixture into a mound. Sprinkle with parsley. Refrigerate until serving. Serve with rye or pumpernickel.

When Tartare is exposed to air it turns to an unappetizing color. Serve only half at a time.

OYSTER CRACKERS

1 1-ounce package Ranch dry dressing mix
¾ cup vegetable oil
2 Tablespoons dried dill
1 Tablespoon lemon pepper
1 10-ounce package oyster crackers
1 9½-ounce package goldfish

Combine dry mix, oil, dill and pepper. Pour mixture over crackers and goldfish. Toss to coat. Spread mixture onto a baking sheet. Bake at 325 degrees 1 hour. Store in an airtight container.

COCKTAIL WIENERS

My little grandchildren always love this! Cute and fun for your Halloween parties.

3   12-ounce jars apple jelly or marmalade
3   9-ounce jars mustard
3   16-ounce packages wieners

Combine jelly and mustard in a saucepan. Cook and stir over low heat until jelly is dissolved. Cut wieners into bite size pieces. Add to mixture. Simmer 2 hours. Pour into casserole dish and serve with toothpicks.

Easy to prepare ahead and reheat.

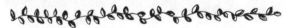

Years ago, when Princess Dianna married Prince Charles, "The Cotton Country Collection" committee sent them our book for a wedding present. We just knew the first thing she would cook for Prince Charles was "Cocktail Weiners".

POCKET PITA BREAD STRIPS

1   10-ounce package pita bread, split open
    Butter, melted
    Lemon pepper to taste

Brush each slice with butter. Sprinkle generously with pepper. Cut into strips. Bake at 325 degrees 1 hour or until dry. Store in an airtight container.

HOT CHEESE PUFFS

Pretty and good for your luncheons!

4 ounces cream cheese, softened
¾ teaspoon grated onion
¼ cup mayonnaise
1 Tablespoon chopped chives
⅛ teaspoon cayenne pepper
2 Tablespoons Parmesan cheese, grated
½ loaf thick white sandwich bread

Combine cream cheese, onions, mayonnaise, chives, pepper and cheese. Cut 2-3 rounds from each bread slice. Spread mixture over each slice. Bake at 350 degrees 15 minutes. May freeze rounds on a cookie sheet. Store in a zip lock bag.

Double cream cheese mixture for one bread loaf.

SAUSAGE CHEESE BISCUITS

An oldie but goodie!

1 8-ounce package shredded extra sharp Cheddar cheese
1 pound package hot bulk pork sausage
2 cups biscuit baking mix
Cayenne pepper to taste, optional

Combine cheese, sausage, baking mix and pepper. Mix well. Drop mixture on ungreased baking sheet. Bake at 400 degrees until browned. Serve hot.

Biscuits freeze well. Reheat in oven.

Salads & Soups

CREATIVE SALADS

The first thing is to invest in a really good salad spinner. The secret of any good salad is to have the greens washed, dried and as cold as possible. You can put the greens in a pillow case with lots of paper towel, refrigerate until ready to serve.

Iceberg Lettuce Wedge Salad

When ICEBERG LETTUCE is fresh and good it is hard to beat. It should be washed and as dry as possible and really ice cold.

Take a large head and cut it into 4 wedges. Cover with damp paper towel and then wrap tightly in wax paper. Refrigerate it until ready to serve. You can buy a good blue cheese dressing and doctor it up with crumbled Maytag Blue Cheese or Kraft, a little fresh ground black pepper and a little lemon juice.

When ready to serve, place lettuce wedges on individual, chilled, salad plates (I put mine in the freezer). Top with blue cheese dressing and garnish with crumbled bacon and finely chopped fresh tomatoes.

Fried Oyster Salad

Have several bags of the GOURMET SALAD MIX ready to go in a big bowl, chilling in the refrigerator. You can use your favorite salad dressing or the BABY BLUE GOURMET SALAD DRESSING is good. Just before serving fry your oysters, drain on lots of paper towel. Mix salad with dressing. NEVER add too much dressing, you do not want the salad SWIMMING in the DRESSING. Add just enough to coat the salad greens.

Top each individual plate with several hot fried oysters and top with a good dollop of TARTAR SAUCE. Serve immediately. That is so good, a little last minute trouble but well worth the extra effort! You must be organized. Do as much ahead as possible.

(Creative Salads, continued)

A quick easy TARTAR SAUCE is about 1½ cups mayonnaise, ½ cup mustard. 1 Tablespoon fresh lemon juice, about ¼ cup finely chopped dill pickle, 2 green onions finely chopped, a little fresh chopped parsley and a Tablespoon or so of capers. You can do this several days ahead.

You could use FRIED OKRA or GRILLED CHICKEN or maybe left over GRILLED STEAK.

BABY BLUE GOURMET SALAD

So wonderful and an absolutely beautiful presentation! VICTOR CASCIO's is the best. MARIE, Victor's wife, makes stuffed artichokes and they are to die for. This is a family of fantastic cooks. Their restaurant, The Chateau, is a North Louisiana favorite.

Dressing:

½   **cup white vinegar**
1   **Tablespoon salt**
½   **teaspoon sugar**
1   **teaspoon pepper**
1   **Tablespoon Dijon mustard**
1   **Tablespoon mayonnaise**
2   **garlic cloves, crushed**
   Zest of 1 lemon
   Juice of 1 lemon
1   **cup olive oil**
½   **cup vegetable oil**

Whisk together the first 8 ingredients. Pour in a jar, add oil and shake well. Be sure and put the top on, dum dum! (Just kidding) Check seasonings. I like to use a big plastic mayonnaise jar to store the dressing, it keeps well in the refrigerator and I have it at all times. This dressing is as important as having fresh milk, bread, butter or eggs! Good on everything but desserts!

(Baby Blue Gourmet Salad, continued)

Salad:

½ **cup sugar**
2 **cups pecans, coarsely
     chopped**
1 **pound spring mix
     salad greens**
1 **pound baby leaf
     spinach**
1 **cup finely chopped
     red onion**
2 **cups fresh
     blueberries, pears
     or strawberries**
¾ **cup Maytag Blue
     cheese, crumbled**

Place sugar in the bottom of a heavy small skillet and heat over medium-high heat until sugar completely melts. Remove from heat. Be careful; sugar burns easily. Stir in pecans to coat. Pour on a lightly buttered piece of foil. When cool, break into small pieces. You can do this a couple of days ahead.

In a large wooden bowl, toss greens, spinach, onion, blueberries, blue cheese and nuts. Be sure and have everything ice cold. Add enough salad dressing to coat. You never want your salad swimming in dressing! Check seasonings and serve immediately on chilled salad plates. Garnish with a blue or purple pansy or a big fresh strawberry.

PANZANELLA

Do not bother making this traditional Tuscan appetizer unless you get delicious vine ripe tomatoes. This Tuscan Bread Salad is a summer time special!

½ **baguette or good country style bread, cut into ½-inch cubes**
¾ **cup olive oil**
3 **garlic cloves, finely chopped**
3 **to 4 cups chopped fresh tomatoes, juice also**
2 **Tablespoons red wine vinegar**
   Salt and garlic powder to taste
1 **handful basil, torn**

Place bread on a baking sheet. Drizzle olive oil over all and toss (sometimes I add just a pat of melted butter, gives it that good flavor). In a 325 degree oven, toast until crispy. Set aside until ready to serve. In a large salad bowl, just before serving add the rest of the ingredients and toss. Check seasonings. You may need to add a little more olive oil.

ANNA CLAIR SEYMOUR, one of the best cooks around, served this for lunch to our investment club, along with COLD POACHED CHICKEN BREAST with TUNA BASIL SAUCE (pg. 65). Outstanding! I won't name names but I saw several of the old girls going back for thirds. I, probably, was one of them.

I love to receive sincere compliments and I love to give them! DR. ARMAND McHENRY and his beautiful, fun wife JUNE, went on a wonderful river boat cruise. When asked if the food was any good, he said "it was like eating at Anna Claire Seymours every night!

WEST INDIES SALAD

I always think of CATHY and RONNIE MYRICK on this one. After Ivan the terrible, Mike and I motored down to Florida to check on things. Being homeless, we arrived on the Myricks doorstep and were welcomed with a wonderful cold glass of Pinot Grigio and this crabmeat. It was served on a nice crispy cracker. Talk about feeling welcomed! The sweetness of people warms your heart!

1 **large sweet onion, chopped**
1 **pound lump crabmeat, cleaned**
   Salt and pepper to taste
½ **cup vegetable or olive oil**
⅓ **cup cider vinegar**
½ **cup crushed ice**
   Leaf lettuce

Layer half onions on the bottom of a mixing bowl. Top with crabmeat. Layer remaining onions. Sprinkle with salt and pepper. Pour on oil and vinegar. Cover with ice and refrigerate a few hours. The flavors will intensify the longer it is refrigerated. Serve over leaf lettuce.

May add ½ cup sugar to chopped onions and cover with cold water. Let marinate 2 hours. Drain when ready to use. This gives a nice, sweet taste and knocks out the bitter hot taste that some onions have.

SPINACH SALAD

BARBARA CATTAR and PAT WOLFF make the very best salads! Whenever there is an occasion for a big gathering and a salad is needed, they always volunteer! As you know, a really wonderful salad takes time.

Dressing:

½   cup olive oil
¼   cup balsamic vinegar
¼   cup packed brown
       sugar
½   teaspoon sugar
½   teaspoon salt
½   teaspoon paprika
¼   teaspoon dry mustard
½   teaspoon pepper
½   medium sweet onion,
       chopped, white or
       purple

Toss spinach and all ingredients. In a quart jar, mix the dressing and shake really well. Check for seasonings. When ready to serve, pour over well chilled salad.

Salad:

1½ pounds spinach, torn
1½ cups sliced
       mushrooms
½   pound bacon, cooked
       and crumbled
1   11-ounce can
       Mandarin oranges,
       drained
1   large avocado, sliced

Toss spinach with mushrooms, bacon, oranges and avocado. Refrigerate. When ready to serve, pour dressing over salad and toss to coat.

CORNBREAD SALAD

SO COLORFUL AND SO DELICIOUS!

DIANNE`S (I love that name) SOUTHWESTERN CORN-BREAD SALAD was one of the featured recipes in Southern Living. The McCoy family are the proprietors of Melvyn's a local hangout for good burgers and steaks, right here in Monroe.

VERY POPULAR!

1   6-ounce package Mexican cornbread mix
1   1-ounce envelope Ranch dry dressing mix
1   small head Romaine lettuce, shredded
2   large tomatoes, chopped
1   15-ounce can black beans, rinsed and drained
1   15-ounce can whole kernel corn with red and green peppers, drained
1   8-ounce package shredded Mexican four cheese blend
6   bacon slices, cooked and crumbled
5   green onions, chopped, tops and bottoms

Prepare cornbread according to package directions; cool and crumble. Set aside.

Prepare salad dressing according to directions

Layer a large bowl with half each of cornbread, lettuce, and next 6 ingredients; spoon half dressing evenly over the top. Repeat layers with remaining ingredients and dressing. Cover and chill at least 2 hours.

CHEESEBURGER SALAD

All the PLEASURE and good taste and none of the GUILT! A good SUGAR BUSTER hamburger without the bread!

1 large head iceberg lettuce, rinsed, well drained and coarsely chopped
Salt and pepper to taste
1 cup mayonnaise
½ cup prepared mustard
3 to 4 lean hamburger, turkey or soybean patties
3 to 4 slices sharp Cheddar cheese
1 cup cherry tomatoes, halved
1 cup chopped red onion
½ cup chopped dill pickles

In a large salad bowl, place half the lettuce salt and pepper to taste and pour about ⅓ of the mayonnaise mustard over. Cook patties until just done and top with cheese. Cut into bite-sized pieces and layer meat with tomatoes, onion and pickles. Top with remaining lettuce and cover with the rest of the mayo – mustard. Salt and pepper to taste.

This would be fun for a casual lunch and let everyone build their own cheeseburger. You could serve with different kinds of chips.

TOASTED WALNUT BROCCOLI SALAD

This salad is a real crowd pleaser. When you serve this, make several copies of the recipe because everyone is going to want it!

1   cup walnuts or pecans, coarsely chopped
1   package Ramen Noodles, crush with a rolling pin before opening
½   stick butter

Dressing:
1   cup Wesson oil, you can use half olive oil
½   to ¾ cup sugar
½   cup red wine vinegar
3   teaspoons soy sauce

1   large head Romaine Lettuce, torn or cut into bite size pieces
2   cups broccoli, cut into small bite-size pieces
1   cup finely chopped green onions, tops and bottoms

In a small skillet, melt butter and add noodles and nuts, stir until lightly brown. Drain on paper towel. For the dressing, whisk oil, sugar, vinegar and soy sauce. You can do all of this the day before. When ready to serve, in a big wooden bowl, toss lettuce, broccoli and onions.

Toss in toasted noodles and nuts. Add dressing slowly, till all is well coated. Check seasonings, you may need a little salt. Remember, you never want your salad swimming in the dressing! Serve and enjoy!

Caramelized Nuts, Pecans Walnuts and Such: On medium heat, in a small black iron skillet, add ½ cup sugar and stir until sugar melts. Toss in nuts, stirring well. Remove from heat, add ½ cup of boiling water, drain and separate nuts. Set aside until ready to use. The melted sugar gets extremely HOT, be careful and do not burn yourself. It seems it takes forever for a burn to heal, and they are so ugly, and you know we do not like ugly!

WHITE VEGETABLE ASPIC

This so pretty! It is divine and wonderful as a first course for your cocktail buffet served with crackers or toast points.

This is a perfect do ahead recipe!

1   8-ounce package cream cheese, softened, low fat is fine
¼   cup mayonnaise
½   cup Durkee's dressing
2   envelopes gelatin
2   Tablespoons cold water
2   Tablespoons lemon juice
1   15-ounce can baby peas, drained
1   cup canned carrots, drained and chopped
1   12-ounce can asparagus, drained, coarsely chopped, save ¼ cup juice
1   cup finely chopped celery
    Salt and pepper to taste
    Melba rounds or toast points

In a medium bowl, whip cream cheese, mayonnaise and Durkees. Soften gelatin in cold water and lemon juice, dissolve over hot water or in microwave, just a few seconds. Mix well and add to cream cheese mixture. Lightly sprinkle salt and a little red pepper over peas, carrots, asparagus and celery. Fold vegetable mixture into cream cheese mixture and pour in a 1 quart mold or a ring mold is pretty. Serve with Melba rounds or toast points. A slice served on a lettuce leaf makes a pretty salad.

You could double this recipe easily, but maybe use only 3 envelopes gelatin.

WALDORF SALAD – AN OCTOBER GREAT!

This is best when the apples are hard, crisp and sweet. This recipe brings back childhood memories.

4   cups diced apples
½   cup golden raisins
½   cup lemon juice
1   cup chopped celery
1½ cups chopped pecans
    Mayonnaise and salt
      to taste
    Lettuce cups

Put apples and raisins in a bowl; pour lemon juice over and mix well. Just before serving, drain and combine celery and nuts. Mix in enough mayonnaise to moisten and add salt to taste. Heap mixture in crisp lettuce cups.

ICE COLD WATERMELON SALAD

1   big ice cold sweet
    watermelon
1   cup finely chopped
    red onion
½   cup finely chopped
    green onions, tops
    and bottoms
½   cup finely chopped
    cilantro
½   cup finely chopped
    parsley
1   cup capers, drained
1   cup French dressing
2   Tablespoons
    mayonnaise

Cut melon into big chunks. Remove as many seeds as possible. Drain really well. Add onions, cilantro, parsley and capers. Mix well and refrigerate. When ready to serve, blend dressing and mayonnaise. Drizzle dressing over salad.

This is wonderful with BBQ chicken. Nice, cool and very different and delicious.

APRICOT HOLIDAY BAKE

This is SUSAN SPERRY CAGE'S recipe, one of my favorite sister-in-laws. She has brought this rich buttery fruit bake for several of our family holiday celebrations. It is so good with turkey, ham or roast beef. The flavors mingle with all. Easy and pretty to serve.

1 16-ounce can unpeeled apricots, drained
1 16-ounce can whole cranberry sauce
½ cup packed brown sugar
¼ cup lemon juice
15 buttery round crackers, crushed in a bag
6 Tablespoons butter Cinnamon and nutmeg to taste
½ cup finely chopped pecans

In a buttered baking dish, place drained apricots, half side up. Put a small dollop of cranberry sauce in the center of each apricot. Sprinkle with brown sugar and lemon juice. Top with crushed crackers. Dot with butter, sprinkle with cinnamon and nutmeg and pecans. Bake at 375 degrees, uncovered about 30 minutes.

GRAPEFRUIT SALAD

This recipe was shared by BILL DAVIS's family, who have a big grapefruit and orange orchard in Florida!

Dressing:

1   package Italian dry
        dressing mix
¼   cup olive oil
¼   cup balsamic vinegar
½   cup water
        Juice of 1 lemon
2   Tablespoons sugar
2   teaspoons dry
        mustard

Whisk together dry mix, oil, vinegar, water, juice, sugar and mustard. Refrigerate.

Salad:

1   head Romaine
        lettuce, rinsed and
        dried
¼   medium red onion,
        sliced
1   grapefruit, sectioned
1   red, yellow or bell
        pepper, sliced
½   cup raisins
½   cup pecans
½   cup feta cheese,
        crumbled

Combine lettuce, onions, grapefruit, peppers, raisins, pecans and cheese. When ready to serve, drizzle with dressing. Toss to coat. Top with grilled chicken or shrimp for a luncheon.

ORANGE SALAD OR DESSERT

1   6-ounce package
    orange flavored
    gelatin
1   22-ounce can crushed
    pineapple, reserve
    juice
1   16-ounce can sliced
    peaches, reserve
    juice
¾   cup chopped
    marshmallows or
    mini marshmallows
½   cup sugar
3   Tablespoons
    all-purpose flour
1   cup juice
1   egg, beaten
2   Tablespoons butter
    Sour cream or
    whipped topping

Prepare gelatin according to package directions with hot water and 1 cup juice for cold water. Add fruit and marshmallows. Pour mixture into a 13 x 9 x 2-inch baking dish. Refrigerate until set. Combine sugar, flour, pineapple juice, egg and butter in a saucepan. Cook and stir over low heat until thickened. Spread over gelatin. Refrigerate until well set. Cut into squares and serve with a dollop of sour cream for salad or whipped topping for dessert.

This is a Columbia favorite, compliments of the beautiful LILLIAN RISER GENTRY. Now Monroe's own!

CINNAMON APPLES

An apple a day keeps the doctor away! A favorite of old and young!

Apples
Cinnamon Candies or
  Redhots
Raisins
Butter
Foil

Place each cored apple in center of aluminum foil. Fill hole with a Tablespoon each of cinnamon candies and raisins. Dot with butter and seal in foil.

You can cook these on the grill for about 30 minutes or in a 350 degree oven for 30-40 minutes or until tender.

I love to serve these in the fall with game or pork.

SPICED PICKLED PEACHES

Many years ago, when we were young things and when we were planning our dinners and parties, the old saying was "when in doubt, serve a pickled peach!" Pretty on the plate and goes with just about anything!

1	**13-ounce can whole peaches, the smaller the better**
½	**cup sugar**
½	**cup vinegar**
1	**Tablespoon whole cloves**
1	**teaspoon ground allspice**
¼	**teaspoon curry powder**
1	**teaspoon peppercorns**

Drain peaches, reserving juice. Pour juice and all other ingredients in to a sauce pan and bring to a boil. Lower heat and simmer for about 30 minutes. Place peaches in a large jar and pour juice over, cover and refrigerate. Turn upside down and around occasionally to mingle those flavors with the peaches.

RASPBERRY CONGEALED SALAD

An old family favorite! This is a good do ahead. Such a pretty color and perfect for holiday dinners! I like to make mine in small individual molds and serve on a big platter covered with red tip leaf lettuce. In the middle of the platter have a small bowl with a good mayonnaise dressing!

2　3-ounce packages raspberry flavored gelatin
1　cup boiling water
1　20-ounce can crushed pineapple, undrained
1　16-ounce can whole cranberry sauce
1　cup finely chopped celery
1　cups pecans, coarsely chopped
　Mayonnaise, sour cream and sugar to taste

Mix boiling water with jello. Cool. Add pineapple and juice, cranberry sauce, celery and nuts. Chill. Serve with a mixture of mayonnaise, sour cream and a little sugar.

LIME JELLO SALAD

My sister WENDY BAZE does this best! She also makes the best toast points in the world. Perfect!

2   **3-ounce packages lime flavored gelatin**
1   **cup boiling water**
1   **20-ounce can crushed pineapple, undrained**
1   **cup coarsely chopped pecans**
½   **cup shredded Cheddar cheese**
1   **cup cottage cheese**
½   **cup mayonnaise Lettuce leaves**

Dissolve gelatin in water. Cool. Add pineapple with juice, pecans, cheese, cottage cheese and mayonnaise. Mix well. Pour into an 11 x 7 x 2-inch baking dish. Refrigerate. Cut into squares and place on a bed of iceberg lettuce.

Big Tip! Never use fresh pineapple in a congealed salad. The papain in fresh pineapple will not congeal. It prevents the jelling process. I learned the hard way. They say the papain, in some unripe fruits, is used as a meat tenderizer and in some medicines.

HORSERADISH SAUCE

This is the good creamy one. Serve with a good roast beef or tenderloin and of course your corned beef. When preparing for dinner, a party or a special occasion always do as much ahead as possible! Then you can have more fun!

1   **cup heavy cream**
½   **cup freshly ground horseradish**
⅓   **cup mayonnaise**
1   **teaspoon Colman's dry mustard Generous dash of cayenne pepper**

Whisk together cream, horseradish, mayonnaise, mustard and cayenne. Store in the refrigerator.

LEMON ANCHOVY DRESSING

GABRIELLA ROSSI-ESPAGNET ARMSTRONG, with a name like that, is a marvelous cook. Seriously, she is one of the very best. Having grown up in Europe, she brings a lot of the old world touch to her cooking! Gabriella shared her source, with me, for this wonderful sauce. Don't you just love people who share?

Serve in a bowl surrounded by snow peas in a circular pattern. Garnish with capers. Also good with cucumbers, blanched asparagus and green beans. Great as a sauce for FISH or SHRIMP. I always take this to Florida, as it keeps well in the refrigerator for a week or so. If you are not a big fan of anchovies, you will be after you taste this. This fabulous sauce is out of Monroe's own Junior League cookbook, Celebration On The Bayou, the baby sister to Cotton Country Collection. Both of these books are a must for your cookbook collection!

2 egg yolks	Combine egg yolks, mustard, anchovies, lemon juice, and onions in food processor and mix until smooth. With machine on, slowly add oil. Pour into a bowl and stir in sour cream by hand. Season with salt and pepper. Cover and refrigerate.
3 to 4 Tablespoons Dijon mustard	
1 2-ounce can anchovies, undrained	
Juice of 1 lemon	
1 green onion, finely chopped, top and bottom	
1 cup olive oil	
¼ cup sour cream	
Salt and pepper to taste	

CRESCENT OIL BAR B-QUE SAUCE

When I was a child, my family and spent many happy, fun times at the HAROLD WOODS, SR. camp in Crestwood. This is way out in West Monroe, on the corner of Arkansas and Johnson Road. Back then it seemed it took forever to get there. This was a real camp with a big screened in porch that wrapped around the camp, with lots of swinging beds and huge stone fire place in the big room. It had a wonderful big kitchen, ponds stocked with bass and big bream, horses to ride and great food. The best fried chicken, fresh corn pudding, big platters of sliced tomatoes, peas, you name it. J.T. the cook would charcoal big 3 to 4-inch bone-in sirloin steaks. This is the sauce! I have never forgotten it.

3 **lemons, thinly sliced**
3 **onions, thinly sliced, rings separated**
1 **stick butter**
1 **11-ounce bottle steak sauce**
1 **10-ounce bottle Worcestershire sauce**

Combine all, bring to a slow boil and reduce heat and cook about 20 minutes.

NAVY BEAN SOUP...CAS-CA-RA

We know that beans are wonderful for you and loaded with fiber. So much fiber has been taken out the processed foods that we eat today. There is more diverticulitis, colon cancer, digestive problems maybe stemming from this. "Cascara sagrada" an herb used for its laxative qualities! Anyway, there is a story behind this recipe and we know beans are good for you!

2   **pounds navy beans**
2   **cups chopped onions**
½   **cup chopped bell pepper**
½   **cup chopped celery**
2   **Tablespoons minced garlic**
1   **pound boiled ham, diced**
      Salt, pepper and cayenne pepper to taste
2   **cups diced tomatoes, optional**
      Cornbread

Wash beans well and put in a heavy Dutch oven. Add the rest of ingredients, bring to a boil, reduce heat and simmer until tender. You may need to add more water. Check seasonings. Serve with cornbread.

This is very close to THE FAMOUS SENATE RESTAURANT BEAN SOUP . Mike and I were in Washington for the New Orleans D Day Museum gala. We stayed in the beautiful home, on Capitol Hill, with our family, Senator Mary Landrieu, her husband Frank Snellings and their children Conner and Mary Shannon. We had a wonderful tour of the capitol and lunch at the senate. Washington was rainy and cold and this soup hit the spot!

CHICKEN STOCK

Nothing better than a good homemade chicken stock or broth! Hands down this is the best and it freezes well!

3-4 **pound chicken hen**
4 **quarts water**
3 **cups chopped celery**
1 **large onion, studded with cloves**
2 **carrots, coarsely chopped**
1 **cup coarsely chopped parsley**
½ **teaspoon dried thyme**
2 **Tablespoons salt**
1 **Tablespoon pepper**

In a large pot, cover hen with cold water. And bring to a boil. Add vegetables and seasonings, cover and simmer several hours, or more, until the leg will pull off easily. Strain, cool slightly and place stock in the refrigerator. When stock is cool, remove the fat. Now you have a wonderful HOMEMADE CHICKEN STOCK.

Save the chicken for salads or CHICKEN DIANNE or what about KING RANCH CHICKEN or better yet CHICKEN ENCHILADAS BUTTA MARIA!

HOT TOMATO PUNCH

Perfect to pass in demitasse cups for a brunch or luncheon! Pretty too and oh, so good!

1 **quart Bloody Mary mix**
2 **cups tomato sauce**
¼ **cup lemon juice**
¼ **cup Worcestershire sauce or vinegar**
Tabasco sauce and salt to taste
Unsweetened whipped cream

Mix all ingredients except whipped cream. Heat. Serve in demitasse cups and top with a dollop of whipped cream.

CURRIED PUMPKIN SOUP

LOVE TO SERVE THIS IN THE FALL OF THE YEAR!

This is Me-J O'Neal's, from Choudrant, and is it good! When the Boys and Girls club of West Monroe were in need of a gas grill I called the John O'Neal's, of O'Neal Gas, and it was there in a Choudrant second!

2	**Tablespoons butter**
1	**8-ounce package sliced fresh mushrooms**
½	**cup chopped onion**
2	**Tablespoons all-purpose flour**
1	**Tablespoon curry powder**
3	**cups chicken broth**
2	**cups canned pumpkin**
1	**Tablespoon honey**
½	**teaspoon salt**
¼	**teaspoon ground nutmeg**
¼	**teaspoon pepper**
1	**12-ounce can evaporated milk**
	Garnish: sour cream and chopped chives

Melt butter in a large saucepan; add mushrooms and onions, sauté until tender. Stir in flour and curry powder; gradually add chicken broth, and cook over medium heat, stirring constantly, until thoroughly heated. Always check seasonings. Garnish and serve.

Tips:

You can use sweet potatoes and or sweet potatoes and pumpkin mixed are good.

Try a little red pepper and maybe a little more curry.

You know I like a homemade, defatted, chicken stock, but the can is really good too.

SPINACH BISQUE

I think this is better, made several days ahead; the flavors have time to mingle. For a wonderful variation add a can of artichokes, but be sure to check for tough leaves on the or fresh sliced mushrooms, drained and sautéed in a little butter.

6   **Tablespoons butter**
1   **cup chopped onion**
¼   **cup all-purpose flour**
3   **cups chicken broth**
3   **cups evaporated milk**
1   **cup whipping cream**
2   **10-ounce packages frozen chopped spinach, cooked but not drained**
    Salt, pepper and cayenne to taste
2   **Tablespoons Pernod, optional**
    Garnish: Grated nutmeg
    Toast points

In a Dutch oven, melt butter and sauté onions until tender. Add flour and stir until bubbly. Add broth and milks slowly, stirring to make a sauce. Add spinach and simmer 5 to 10 minutes, stirring to blend. Remove from heat. Add salt and pepper. Check seasonings.

Serve with homemade toast points.

When reheating or heating, be sure and heat very slowly, watch carefully or heat over a pan of hot water... the French call it BAIN MARIE! Hot water bath! If not, it might curdle!

Just a little trivia about PERNOD. It was made with absinthe which was wormwood or its essence. It is a green bitter liqueur with the flavor of licorice and anise. They say Vincent Van Gough was addicted to absinthe and died of absinthism.

CABBAGE SOUP

Nothing tastes as good as thin feels! This is a FAT BURNING SOUP! You can eat it all day long and as much as you want. If you really want to lose weight, try 3 or 4 days of just this soup, you will be amazed! The only bad thing is you will never like cabbage again! Just kidding! DEFINITE NO NO`S... ALCOHOL, SWEETS, PASTA, RICE, POTATOES, CORN, BREAD, BEETS and CARROTS. Remember: nothing white...except maybe cauliflower.

1½ **cups water**
1 **large head cabbage, coarsely chopped**
1 **bunch green onions, chopped tops and bottoms**
2 **bell peppers, chopped**
1-2 **10-ounce cans diced tomatoes with green chilies**
1 **bunch celery, chopped**
1 **cup chopped parsley**
1 **package onion soup mix**
Salt, pepper, curry powder and cayenne pepper to taste

In a large pot, add about 1½ cups water and bring to a boil, add cabbage and cook about 5 minutes. Add all other ingredients, bring to a boil, cut to simmer and continue cooking until vegetables are tender.

Eat as much as you want, whenever you are hungry, anytime of the day. This soup will not add calories; the more you eat the more you lose. If eaten alone for indefinite periods, you would suffer from malnutrition. The GOOD NEWS is after 3 or 4 days you can add fruit, a little brown rice, squash, chicken, steak maybe a small baked potato. Be sure and keep this soup in the refrigerator and heat just what you are eating at the time.

VIRGINIA PEANUT SOUP

Peanut soup is to Virginia what white bean soup is to Boston! Really different and really good!

2   quarts chicken broth
1   small onion, diced
1   stick butter
1   pint peanut butter
2   stalks celery, diced
3   Tablespoons flour
½   teaspoon celery salt
1   teaspoon salt
1   Tablespoon lemon
      juice
    Ground peanuts
    Parsley and green
      onions, finely
      chopped

Melt butter in a Dutch oven, add onion and celery. Sauté for 5 minutes, but do not brown. Add flour and mix well. Add hot chicken broth and cook for ½ hour. Remove from stove, strain and add peanut butter, celery salt and lemon juice. Just before serving, sprinkle with ground peanuts, parsley and green onions.

Mike and I were in Middleburg, Virginia in early December. It started snowing and we felt like we were in a Currier and Ives Christmas card. The little town was in a hustle and bustle preparing for the holiday parade. The fox hunters, horses and dogs were in full regalia. We stopped at the RED FOX INN, for lunch, and had a ring side seat in front of a big roaring fire and enjoyed this soup and the parade.

CORN AND GREEN CHILE CHOWDER

If ever you are in Northern New Mexico in the early fall, you will know it by the intoxicating smell of roasting Hatch chilies. Be sure to pick up a bushel and find out how to roast them. You will, for sure, be spoiled by the wonderful flavor and taste. Both the soup and the Hatch chilies freeze well.

4	Tablespoons butter
1½	cups finely chopped green onions, tops and bottoms
2	slices bacon, chopped
4	cups fresh or frozen corn
1	cup chopped green chilies
1	Tablespoon all-purpose flour
3-4	cups hot chicken broth
1	teaspoon salt
1	teaspoon pepper
½	teaspoon cayenne pepper
¼	teaspoon dried thyme
2	cups heavy cream Garnish: chopped green onions, green chilies or crumbled bacon

In a Dutch oven over medium heat, cook onions in butter and bacon about 10 minutes or until soft. Add corn and chilies, sprinkle flour, mix well and slowly cook 2 or 3 minutes. Add broth, seasonings and cream. Simmer, slowly, stirring occasionally, so as not to curdle. Check seasonings. If something is missing it is usually salt and red pepper.

Serve in pretty bowls and garnish with a few chopped green onions, green chilies or crumbled crispy bacon bits. Not the kind in the jar, the one you fry!

(Corn and Green Chile Chowder, continued)

Tips:

You can substitute fresh LUMP Crabmeat for the chilies or a little of both. A little chopped ham is good, mixed in. If you are lucky enough to have HATCH GREEN CHILIES, you are in for a real treat!

You know this would be a tad better with a good well seasoned, homemade, chicken stock that you have defatted.

I love to use the Land of the Lakes FAT FREE half-and-half. So good and it cooks and taste just like real heavy cream or half-and-half.

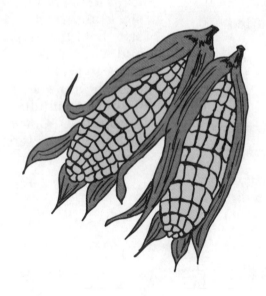

SHRIMP POSOLE

This soup is especially great for cool weather because the spices keep you warm. Tomatillos generally are easy to find at the grocery. We have so many things available in our markets now that we did not have before. These little green tomatillos are fun to cook with, flavors of Mexico and New Mexico!

2 **pounds tomatillos, husked**
1 **cup chopped green chilies**
   Olive oil
2 **medium onions, minced**
3 **garlic cloves, minced**
1 **teaspoon ground cumin**
1 **teaspoon ground coriander**
1 **teaspoon dried oregano**
   Salt and cayenne pepper to taste
2 **15½-ounce cans hominy**
6 **cups chicken broth**
2 **cups corn**
   Olive oil
   Chopped cilantro
1½ **pounds shrimp**
   Avocado, sliced
1 **to 2 limes, cut into wedges**
   4 tortillas, cut into strips and fried in oil

Put tomatillos in boiling water and simmer until soft about 10 minutes. Strain and add to food processor with chilies and purée.

Heat oil in a large pot, add onions and cook until soft. Add garlic and cook 5 minutes. Add seasonings and cook 1 minute. Add tomatillos purée, hominy, chicken stock and corn. Bring to a slow boil, then reduce heat and simmer about 15 minutes. To serve, reheat stew, add shrimp and cook 5 or 6 more minutes. Check seasonings. Garnish with avocado, lime wedges and shredded fried tortillas.

OYSTER STEW

This was my DADDY`S favorite and my GRANDMOTHER, LELA KING, made it best! Only serve oysters in the R months; the waters are cold and they are BEST!

4   Tablespoons butter
1   Tablespoon all-purpose flour
1   small bunch green onions, chopped, tops and bottoms
4   cups warm milk
2   stalks celery, finely chopped
4   whole cloves
    Salt, white pepper and cayenne pepper to taste
    Worcestershire sauce to taste
3   dozen oysters and liquor

Make a light roux of the butter and flour. Add onions and cook for a short time. Heat milk separately; add to roux. Add celery, cloves and seasonings. Cook slowly. Be careful and do not curdle it. When thickened add oysters and a little of the liquor. Do not boil. Serve very hot. Remove cloves before serving. Serve with buttered, toasted saltine crackers that have cooled slightly. A fresh, cold green salad is nice with this.

Tip:

Check oysters for shells. Heat soup in a water bath, (a method of cooking delicate mixtures by setting the dish in a roasting pan of water in the oven.) I do mine in a big skillet with water, on top of the stove, so as not to curdle. The French would say Bain Marié, water bath.

CHEESE SOUP

This recipe was given to me by Pat Evans and was served at one of the most beautiful luncheons on Lake D'Arbonne at the summer home of my friend NITA THOMAS. Everything was perfect but this soup was really good. Those Ruston ladies, JOANN BARHAM, ROBERTA HINTON, BERVERLY JAMES, I wish I could name them all, know how to give the perfect luncheon and make you feel special!

3 carrots, finely chopped
3 stalks celery, finely chopped
1 large onion, finely chopped
4 Tablespoons butter
2 15-ounce cans chicken broth
2 10¾-ounce cans cream of potato soup
1 pound processed cheese loaf, cut into cubes
1 8-ounce container sour cream
   Salt and cayenne pepper to taste
   Garnish: Finely chopped parsley

Sauté carrots, celery and onion in butter. Add 2 cans of broth and simmer uncovered for 30 minutes. Add potato soup and cheese. Simmer 10 minutes. Stir in sour cream just before serving. Garnish with parsley.

Easy to double or triple.

Free
Range

ORIENTAL CHICKEN

Perfect for a brunch or lunch! Serve over my cheese soufflé (Cooking & Gardening, pg. 105). MOST DELICIOUS!

1	**stick butter**
½	**cup all-purpose flour**
1	**Tablespoon salt**
1	**cup heavy cream**
2	**cups warm whole milk**
2	**cups hot chicken broth**
2	**cups large diced chicken**
½	**cup mushrooms, sauteed in butter**
½	**cup blanched almonds**
1	**cup sliced water chestnuts**
¼	**cup pimento**
¼	**cup sherry**

Melt butter in a large skillet, add flour and salt and cool until bubbly; add cream slowly, stirring well. When it is fairly thick slowly add warm milk and hot stock, whisking until smooth. You may need a little more stock. Cook over hot water for about 30 minutes. Add rest of the ingredients. Serve with fresh steamed asparagus and a grilled tomato.

COLD POACHED CHICKEN BREASTS WITH TUNA BASIL SAUCE

ANNA CLAIR SEYMOUR served this for lunch at our Investment Club Meeting. All eighteen went back for seconds and thirds. IT'S THAT GOOD!

3   large whole chicken breasts with skin and bone, about 1¼ pounds each
    Salt and pepper to taste
1   6½-ounce can tuna packed in olive oil, well drained
½   cup mayonnaise
¼   cup plain yogurt
3   anchovy filets
1   Tablespoon capers, drained plus more for garnish
2   Tablespoons lemon juice or to taste
⅓   cup finely chopped basil leaves plus 6 sprigs for garnish
    Garnish: Lemon slices
    Mixture of Niçoise and Kalamata olives

Place chicken in a large stockpot. Add enough cold water to cover by 1-inch. Remove chicken. Bring to boil. Add salt, pepper and chicken. Reduce heat and poach chicken 18 minutes. Remove from heat. Cool chicken in liquid 30 minutes. Drain chicken and let stand until cool enough to handle. Discard skin and bones, being careful to remove breast half in one piece. Wrap in plastic wrap and refrigerate at least 6 hours or overnight.

Combine tuna, mayonnaise, yogurt, anchovies, capers, juice, salt and pepper in a food processor. Process until smooth. Transfer sauce to an airtight container. Refrigerate at least 6 hours or overnight.

To serve, cut chicken breasts diagonally into ¼-inch slices. Transfer a breast to each of 6 dinner plates. Just before serving, add basil to sauce. Spoon sauce over chicken. Garnish with capers, basil sprigs and lemon slices. Serve with olives.

CHICKEN N' DUMPLINS

Just for SALLIE JAYNE SNELLINGS!

This is the easy way! Even Queen Elizabeth would fall out over this fabulous, old fashioned dish! Perfect for an elegant dinner party or country supper! You set the stage! The secret is the hen and the stock that it makes and the fat or schmaltz I asked my old friend, cook, bottle washer and helper Rosalee why a hen made such a difference and she said "maybe it's 'cause it's been around so long, it knows all da secrets!" Sounds good to me!

1	**large old hen**
1	**onion, chopped**
2	**celery ribs, chopped**
1	**or 2 hot peppers, chopped**
2	**bay leaves**
½	**cup parsley chopped**
	Salt and lots of black pepper
3	**packages Mary B's Open Kettle Dumplings**

If you do not have a large stock pot, I recommend a 12 quart Magnalite; it is perfect for gumbos and such!

The DAY BEFORE, in your large pot cover hen with water add all ingredients, bring to a boil, reduce heat and cook slowly for 4 or 5 hours or until that old bird is tender. Remove hen from stock and bone out the meat, put in a bowl, cover and refrigerate. Cool stock in pot and place in the ice box until the next day or 2.

We are having Chicken n' Dumplings tonight! Get that pot out of the ice box and remove all that beautiful yellow fat or SCHMALTZ except for about ½ cup. Leave that; it is the good part. Bring the stock and fat to a boil. Follow the directions

(Chicken n' Dumplins, continued)

on the frozen dumplings package. I cook mine about an hour, add the chicken, cook slowly about 30 more minutes turn the heat off and let them sit 1 or 2 hours before serving. They have time to absorb the stock and plump up. They will stay plenty warm and ready to serve!

Serve with sweet potatoes, purple hull peas or green peas, a hot fruit bake or fresh fruit is wonderful, thick slices of fresh tomatoes, if they are in season and hot cornbread! For dessert let's have, you got it, BANANA PUDDING!

Schmaltz, the Yiddish way or Schmalz, the German way, is rendered fat from the hen! All the good flavor is there. You just have to have a little bit in your Dumplings, Matzo Ball Soup and of course Cornbread Dressing! A little bit of the fat will not hurt you and you are not going to eat the whole thing! I throw most of it away but there are places that sell it, it is like gold!

AUSTRIAN CHICKEN STRUDEL

This is an easy but elegant way to serve chicken. Garnish each serving with a dollop of sour cream and fresh rosemary sprig!

4   green onions, finely chopped
⅓   pound mushrooms, sliced
2   Tablespoons butter
4   cups cooked cubed chicken
½   teaspoon salt
¼   teaspoon pepper
2   Tablespoons chopped parsley
½   teaspoon dried tarragon
2   eggs, beaten
1½ cups grated Swiss cheese
1   16-ounce package frozen phyllo pastry, use 16 sheets
1   stick butter, melted
    Garnish: Sour cream

Saute onions and mushrooms in butter until tender. Combine mixture with chicken, salt, pepper, parsley and tarragon. Stir in eggs and cheese. Brush one pastry sheet with butter. Place a second sheet on top and brush with butter. Spoon ⅔ cup chicken filling along one end of the rectangle, leaving a 2-inch margin from the end and both sides. Fold in ends and loosely roll up pastry. Brush with butter and place on a greased baking sheet seam side down. Repeat with remaining pastry and chicken filling. Bake at 400 degrees 35 minutes or until crust is golden brown. Top with sour cream.

CHICKEN ROLL

Virginia and Thomas love this one!

1 can, crescent rolls
1 cup, cut-up chicken
1 small can mushrooms
1 3-ounce package
   cream cheese
¼ cup dry parsley
½ teaspoon salt
½ teaspoon lemon
   pepper
½ teaspoon red pepper
2 Tablespoons butter
1 cup seasoned bread
   crumbs

Mix cream cheese, butter, salt, pepper, parsley and lemon pepper thoroughly. Stir in chicken and chopped mushrooms. Spread on crescent rolls. Roll up from wide end.

Dip the rolls in melted butter and roll in bread crumbs. Bake on an ungreased cookie sheet for about 25 minutes.

CHICKEN ENCHILADAS BUTTA MARIA

A real crowd pleaser! My sister BERTHA MARIE (Rebo) is famous for the enchiladas. When you fix this, make plenty of copies of the recipe because everyone is going to want one.

1 3-pound chicken or 4 boneless, skinless chicken breast halves
1 large onion, chopped Olive oil
1 10¾-ounce can cream of chicken soup
2 10-ounce cans tomatoes with green chilies, drained
   Salt and pepper to taste
1 Tablespoons ground cumin
1 8-ounce container sour cream
12 flour tortillas
4 8-ounce packages Monterey Jack cheese, shredded
1 8-ounce package shredded Cheddar cheese

Steam chicken in salted water until tender. Bone out and cut up. Sauce is prepared by sautéing onion in a small amount of cooking oil, until clear. Add soup, tomatoes, salt and pepper and cumin. Simmer 20 minutes. Remove from heat and add sour cream. In a 13x9x2-inch casserole, spoon a little of the sauce over the bottom of the dish to just cover. Toss chicken with Jack cheese. Fill tortilla shells with the chicken cheese mixture. Roll up and place in dish, seam side down. Pour sauce all over and top with grated Cheddar cheese. Bake covered, 350 degrees about 30 to 45 minutes or until cheeses melt. Serves 6 to 8. You can cut these down the middle before cooking for smaller size.

(Chicken Enchiladas Butta Maria, continued)

Variation: You can use the soft corn tortillas. Fry them in about ¼-inch cooking oil, just a few seconds on each side. They should not be crisp. Drain on paper towels. In a 13x9x2-inch casserole, spread just a little sauce over the bottom and layer tortillas, chicken- cheese mixture. Two layers will be ample. Pour sauce all over and top with 2 cups grated sharp Cheddar cheese. You can add chopped green chilies or chopped jalapeños or for a little more zip, or a sprinkle of red pepper.

CHICKEN-ON-A-STICK

Messy, but worth the trouble!

10 6-inch wooden skewers
2 large white onions, quartered
1 32-ounce jar hamburger dill chip pickles
8 large boneless, skinless chicken breast halves, cut into 1½-inch pieces
1 pound all-purpose flour
2 Tablespoons baking powder
  Salt, pepper and Cajun seasoning
1 quart milk
2 eggs, beaten
1 gallon vegetable oil

Assemble each skewer as follows, onion, pickle, chicken, pickle, onion, pickle, chicken, pickle, onion, pickle, chicken, pickle and onion. It is very important that you put the pickle next to the chicken. Leave room on the ends to handle. Combine flour, baking powder, salt, pepper and Cajun seasoning. In a large bowl, whisk together milk and eggs. Heat oil to 325 degrees. Dip skewers in milk wash and dredge in flour mixture. Fry until golden brown.

BREAKFAST CASSEROLE

Mike and I went to one of the most delightful brunches at the beautiful home of CAYCE and RYAN SARTOR in Frenchman's Bend. Ryan is a master builder and their home reflects Cacye's good taste. They were gracious enough to share their recipes. I could have gone back for thirds.

2½ cups seasoned or
    herbed croutons,
    6-ounce box
1 8-ounce package
    shreddedsharp
    Cheddar cheese
1½ pounds bulk Italian
    sausage, cooked
    and drained
6 eggs
2¼ cups milk
1 teaspoon dry mustard
½ teaspoon pepper
1 10¾-ounce can
    cream of mushroom
    soup
½ cup milk
½ teaspoon cayenne
    pepper, optional

In a 9x13 inch lightly greased casserole dish, place the croutons, then cheese, then sausage that you have browned and drained well. Beat eggs and add milk, mustard and pepper. Pour over the layers. Refrigerate, covered over night. Just before serving dilute the soup with milk. Add pepper and pour over. Bake in a 300 degrees over for 1 hour.

Look on page 93 for GREEN BEANS MARINATED for what was served with this casserole! Each dish complimented the other. A wonderful blend of flavors!

Most casseroles are best taken out of the oven after done, loosely covered and let sit 10 minutes or so. Even when they reach room temperature they are still good.

(Breakfast Casserole, continued)

When planning a big party, your menu should stand on its own, even when it has been sitting out for say an hour or so. You do not want to serve something that requires lots of attention. When the masses arrive, keeping the table cleaned, trays and dishes full is plenty enough to do. Be sure and have someone assigned to picking up drink glasses, napkins, a broken wine glass, spills, etcetera, etcetera. You have worked very hard and YOU WANT TO HAVE FUN TOO!

EGGS À LA CREAM FLORENTINE

2	10-ounce packages frozen chopped spinach
2	Tablespoons all-purpose flour
3	Tablespoons butter Salt, pepper, cayenne pepper, lemon juice, ground nutmeg to taste
6	Tablespoons heavy cream
6	eggs

Cook spinach according to package directions. Save ½ cup liquor. Mix liquor and flour to make a paste. Combine spinach, butter and enough paste to make it creamy. Add salt, pepper, cayenne, juice and nutmeg. Pour mixture into a shallow baking dish. Make six indentations in the spinach. Add one Tablespoon of cream to each well. Break an egg over each well. Bake at 350 degrees 20 minutes or until white is set.

This is wonderful with broiled tomatoes, ham, good English muffins and Mayhaw jelly. You could top these eggs with a dollop of Hollandaise sauce.

DEVILED EGGS

Some folks call them stuffed eggs. MAMA always called them deviled. Either way, they are wonderful and perfect for almost any occasion! According to that wonderful little book "Being Dead Is No Excuse" by Gayden Metcalf and Charlottte Hays, you cannot have a funeral in the Deep South without Stuffed Eggs! If you have not read the book, get it. It is just darling. I laughed until my sides hurt.

1	**dozen hard-boiled eggs**
½	**cup finely chopped dill pickle**
½	**cup finely chopped celery**
¼	**cup mayonnaise**
¼	**cup mustard**
	Salt and pepper to taste
	Dry parsley
	Paprika

Peel hard-boiled eggs and cut in half length-wise. Remove yolks and mash. Add pickles, celery, mayonnaise and mustard. Mix well and season to taste with salt and pepper. Garnish with parsley and paprika.

You can use sweet pickles instead of dill, whatever is your choice. For a little different swing, try a can of deviled ham mixed in.

GREEN CHILI AND CORN FRITTATA

This is from Charlie Risien, our San Antonio connection!

2	17-ounce cans whole corn kernels, drained
1	4-ounce can chopped green chilies, drained
1	to 2 chopped hot pepper, optional
1	small sweet red pepper, cut into thin strips
1	small yellow pepper, cut into thin strips
1	large onion, sliced
3	garlic cloves, minced
¼	cup finely chopped cilantro
2	Tablespoons olive oil
6	eggs
2	to 2½ teaspoons salt
1	teaspoon pepper
1	teaspoon cayenne pepper
½	teaspoon ground cumin
¼	teaspoon chili powder
8	thin bread slices, cubed
1	8-ounce package cream cheese, cubed
1	8-ounce package shredded sharp Cheddar cheese

Grease a 10-inch spring-form pan. Saute corn, chilies, hot peppers, sweet peppers, yellow peppers, onions, garlic and cilantro in oil until tender. Whisk together eggs, salt, pepper, cayenne, cumin, chili powder, half the bread, cream cheese and Cheddar cheese. Stir in vegetables. Mix well. Press remaining bread into the bottom of pan. Pour mixture over bread. Place pan on a foil-lined baking sheet. Bake at 350 degrees 55 minutes or until set. Cool slightly before serving.

This is good for a weekend brunch or Sunday supper. I like to serve fresh sliced tomatoes with goat cheese and fresh chopped basil.

CHEDDAR CHEESECAKE

1½ Tablespoons butter,
for pan
¼ cup fine
breadcrumbs,
lightly toasted
¼ cup shredded sharp
Cheddar cheese
6 ounces ham, thinly
sliced or crawfish
1 8-ounce package
cream cheese,
softened
1 12-ounce package
shredded sharp
Cheddar cheese
1 cup cottage cheese
¾ cup chopped green
onions
4 eggs
3 Tablespoons finely
chopped jalapeño
pepper, seeded
2 Tablespoons milk
1 garlic clove, halved

Butter a 9-inch springform pan. Combine breadcrumbs and cheese. Sprinkle into pan, turning to coat. Refrigerate. Dice half the ham, reserve remaining slices. Combine diced ham, cream cheese, Cheddar cheese, cottage cheese, onions, eggs, peppers, milk and garlic in a food processor. Purée until smooth. Pour more than slightly half filling into pan. Top with reserved ham slices in an even layer. Cover with remaining filling. Set pan on a baking sheet. Bake at 325 degrees 1 hour, 15 minutes. Turn off oven and cool cheesecake about 1 hour with door ajar. Cool completely before serving.

May double to serve up to 50.

Breads

TOAST POINTS

For fine entertaining, Toast Points are a must!

1   **stick butter, melted**
2   **to 3 Tablespoons**
      dried parsley
1   **loaf thin Pepperidge**
      Farms
      sliced bread

Combine butter and parsley. Brush bread slices with butter mixture with a pastry brush. Cut each slice into 4 squares or triangles. Place on an ungreased baking sheet. Bake at 250 degrees 1 hour.

Variation: After brushing with butter, sprinkle each slice with Parmesan cheese or lemon pepper. Cut into four long strips and bake until dry and crispy.

MONKEY BREAD

1 **Recipe for Ice Box
Roll, (Cooking and
Gardening, pg. 126)
Melted butter**

Prepare Ice Box Roll *(Cooking & Gardening with Dianne, pg. 126)*, according to recipe directions. Form dough into balls about the size of an English walnut. Dip balls in butter. Place one layer in a well greased tube pan. Continue to layer balls until pan is half full. Let rise 45 minutes. Bake at 375 degrees 45 to 50 minutes.

It is fun to make this in individual ramekins. Layer half full and give each guest his own ramekin of bread. Remember to adjust baking time.

<u>Variation:</u> Dip balls in butter, then in a cinnamon and sugar mixture before baking.

<u>Variation:</u> For dinner bread, dip balls in butter then in a Parmesan cheese and dried parsley mixture.

YEAST BISCUITS

"Talk about" good!

1 package active dry yeast
½ cup warm water
1 egg
½ cup milk
1 Tablespoon sugar
4 Tablespoons butter, melted
3½ cups biscuit baking mix

Dissolve yeast in water. Let sit overnight if possible. Combine egg, milk, sugar and butter. Stir in yeast. Mix well. Gradually add biscuit mix and stir until smooth. Pour dough into a greased bowl. Cover with a towel and let rise about 1 hour. Turn dough out onto a floured surface with a little biscuit mix. Knead biscuit mix into dough until it is not sticky. Roll out dough. Cut with a round biscuit cutter. Place in a greased pan with sides lightly touching. Let rise again for 45 minutes. Bake at 350 degrees 12 to 15 minutes. Serve with creamy butter, Cane Ribbon syrup or Mayhaw jelly.

SOUR CREAM BISCUITS

Nothing better than homemade!

2 cups biscuit baking mix
1 teaspoon dried dill
1 8-ounce container sour cream
1 stick butter, melted

Combine biscuit mix, dill, sour cream and butter. Mix well. Turn dough out onto a lightly floured surface. Knead gently 5 to 6 times. Roll dough to ½-inch thickness. Cut with a 1-inch round cutter. Place on a lightly greased baking sheet. Bake at 450 degrees 6 to 8 minutes or until lightly browned.

HOLIDAY BRAIDED BREAD WITH FRUIT

3   packages active dry yeast
½   cup warm water
1   stick butter, softened
1½ cups sugar
1   teaspoon salt
3   eggs
7   to 8 cups all-purpose flour
1   to 1½ cups milk
    Favorite preserves, or dried fruit. Also, you can use the candied cherries, pineapple, raisins, dates (the fruit cake mixture)
    Toasted pecans, chopped

Dissolve yeast in water. Cream butter, sugar and salt. Stir in yeast. Add eggs alternately with flour and milk. Mix well. May need to add more flour. Switch to a dough hook. Knead 10 minutes. Place dough in a well oiled bowl, turning to coat. Cover with oiled plastic wrap and let rise until double in size. Punch down and divide in half. Divide each half into three equal pieces. Roll out like a sausage. As you are braiding dough, spoon in preserves and try to cover with dough as well as possible. Place on greased baking sheet. Cover loosely with plastic wrap. Let rise. Bake at 350 degrees until golden brown.

Toasting pecans, a little, brings out the flavor.

HOT TOASTY CHEESE LOGS

Better than Bayou DeSiard Country Club. Perfect for a ladies lunch or brunch! Ideal for passing at cocktail parties! No one will pass them up! THEY ARE JUST PLAIN GOOD!

1   **stick butter, melted**
2   **Tablespoons dried parsley**
1   **20-ounce loaf white sandwich bread, crust removed**
1   **12-ounce container pimento cheese**
    Cayenne pepper, parsley and paprika to taste

Melt butter and mix in parsley. Brush one side of the bread with the butter mixture. Turn over and spread half of the slice with about 1 teaspoon or more of the pimento cheese. Sprinkle with red pepper. Roll, like a cigar and press or pinch seam together. Place on a foil lined baking sheet, seam side down. Sprinkle with a little more dried parsley and a little paprika. Bake 350 degrees for about 15 minutes. For smaller logs, you can cut them in half before cooking. They are pretty to pass. These freeze well.

These are perfect with a good chicken salad, deviled eggs, and fresh fruit salad with poppy seed dressing. Ice cream and tea cakes are nice for dessert.

OKRA CORNBREAD

LINDA TATUM from Newellton found this recipe in Louisiana Country Magazine. Her husband loved it so much she shared it with me. Always a good thing to keep our husbands happy!

1   **cup chopped okra**
1   **cup chopped tomatoes**
1   **cup chopped onions**
2   **eggs**
⅓   **cup milk**
1   **9-ounce box cornbread mix**
   Salt and pepper to taste

Combine okra, tomatoes, onions, eggs, milk, cornbread mix, salt and pepper. Mix well. Pour mixture into a greased muffin tin or 7-inch skillet. Dot with butter. Bake at 375 degrees 30 minutes or until browned.

May use leftover stewed okra and tomatoes. It will make the bread a little more browned because the vegetables are cooked.

PIZZA BREAD

This is a neighborhood special! About 28 years ago my son, George was playing with friends on Valencia Avenue. He brought the recipe and samples of the PIZZA BREAD home and it was WONDERFUL! Recently at an afternoon party, I was visiting with a cute group of old friends from the Valencia neighborhood, they started talking about this PIZZA BREAD....Said their families would go into withdrawals when they would get down to the last loaf...I regret that I never prepared this for my little boy...

As they say, it is never too late!

Here is to the PIZZA BREAD QUEENS .... Vonette Wells, Susan Wheeler, Pat Cascio, Gabriella Armstrong, Liz Ormes and Ellen Webb.

6	**loaves frozen bread dough, thawed**
3	**pounds pork sausage**
1	**pound ham, finely chopped**
1	**pound salami, finely chopped**
6	**jalapeños, finely chopped**
2	**6-ounce cans pitted black olives, finely chopped**
1	**ounce jar Italian salad mix, chopped**
2	**cups green onion tops, finely chopped**
1	**12-ounce package shredded Provolone cheese**

Let bread dough rise overnight. Roll out each bread loaf into a rectangle. Brown sausage. Drain well. Add ham, salami, jalapeños, olives, salad mix and green onions. Combine all cheeses. On each rolled out bread, spread a layer of meat mixture. Top with cheese mixture. Roll dough up jelly roll style. The loaves will be rather thick. Bake at 300 degrees 45 minutes. Cut each loaf into ten 1½-inch slices. Sprinkle with cayenne.

(Pizza Bread, continued)

1 8-ounce package
   shredded Swiss
   cheese
1 8-ounce package
   shredded Cheddar
   cheese
1 8-ounce package
   shredded
   mozzarella cheese
1 3-ounce can
   Parmesan cheese
   Cayenne pepper,
   optional

This freezes well but be sure to bake, slice, wrap in heavy duty foil and then freeze. When ready to serve, heat in foil loosely open so it will get hot and crusty brown. May also divide bread dough loaves in half so it is not quite as big.

I know now why I did not make this. This is a lot of stuff and a lot of chopping! Way back then, food processors were not around. This would be great for a really big group, like feeding a senior class or the Youth at your church.

I made 3 big loaves and 6 half loaves, that I thought were prettier and still had a big bowl of the meat and cheese leftover. I was tired of making Pizza Bread. The leftovers are perfect for a build your own Pizza Salad!

NOTES

Vegetables

EGGPLANT, PEPPER, TOMATO, ONION, GARLIC AND HERB BAKE

What is my very favorite vegetable? EGGPLANT!

This is best only in the summer time when everything is garden fresh!

MICHELE, TAYLOR, and JORDAN Favorite!

2	**medium eggplants**
3	**bell peppers, sliced**
3	**to 4 tomatoes, sliced**
2	**to 3 sweet onions, sliced ¼- to ½-inch thick**
3	**to 4 garlic cloves, coarsely chopped**
½	**cup chopped parsley**
¼	**cup chopped oregano**
	Salt, pepper and cayenne pepper to taste
	Olive oil

Cover a large baking sheet with foil and drizzle with a little olive oil. Slice eggplant, bell pepper, tomatoes, and onions, about ¼ to ½ inch thick. Layer on the baking sheet, onions, bell pepper, eggplant and tomatoes. Sprinkle garlic, parsley, oregano, salt and pepper. Drizzle with a little more olive oil. Bake 350 degrees about 1 hour or until eggplant and other vegetables are tender.

I serve this with a thin Angel Hair Pasta, and it is just perfect with pan fried Speckled Trout. This is so wonderful; it would be good with anything but maybe ice cream!

OVEN-FRIED EGGPLANT

This recipe is from ANN LEDOUX, who is a wonderful cook and fabulous gardener!

⅓   **cup fine dry breadcrumbs**
2   **Tablespoons grated Parmesan cheese**
¼   **teaspoon salt**
¼   **teaspoon pepper**
1   **¾-pound eggplant, peeled and cut into ¼-inch slices**
¼   **cup mayonnaise or salad dressing**
  Garnish: Freshly chopped basil

Combine breadcrumbs, cheese, salt and pepper in a shallow dish. Spread both sides of eggplant slices with mayonnaise. Dredge in breadcrumb mixture. Place on a lightly greased baking sheet. Bake at 400 degrees 10 to 12 minutes or until browned. Sprinkle with basil.

STUFFED EGGPLANT PARMESAN

This is absolutely fabulous and an outstanding presentation, and it's so EASY! You can use a spaghetti sauce like Prego from the jar and just doctor it up.

Sauce:

2	Tablespoons olive oil
1	onion, minced
3	cloves garlic, finely chopped
1½	pounds Italian sausage
1	quart can Italian plum tomatoes
1	6 ounce can tomato paste
3	Tablespoons parsley, finely chopped
1	teaspoon oregano
1	Tablespoon salt
1	Tablespoon pepper
1	teaspoon sugar
1	water or chicken stock

Eggplant:

4	to 6 small eggplant
	Olive oil
	Italian seasoning mix
	Salt, pepper and red pepper
	Garlic salt
1½	cups Parmesan or Romano Cheese, grated
2	Tablespoons Italian Breadcrumbs
4	to 6 thin lemon slices

Remove Italian sausage from the casing and cut into cubes about the size of small meatballs. Brown and drain off excess fat. Saute the onion, garlic, salt and meat in olive oil until meat is no longer pink. Add remaining ingredients and simmer, uncovered, about 1 hour. You want most of the water absorbed but not too dry. Check seasonings.

While sauce is simmering, boil whole eggplant until done or until a knife inserts in easily. Gently removed from water, pat dry and cool slightly. Make a small slit in the side of the eggplant and carefully drizzle in olive oil, seasonings, 2 or 3 tablespoons of cheese, a sprinkle of bread crumbs

You can serve slices of the eggplant if they are too big.

(Stuffed Eggplant Parmesan, continued)

and top with lemon. Gently press together and place on top of well-seasoned sauce. Simmer 30-40 minutes.

Each guest gets their own whole stuffed eggplant, so you want them small. Serve over angel hair pasta with a good Italian salad and hot, crusty garlic bread. A good Chianti is perfect with this! (Did you know that Chianti is a district in Tuscany?) This can be made the day before and the sauce freezes well!

GREEK STUFFED EGGPLANT

2	**eggplants**
1	**cup chopped bell pepper**
1	**onion, minced**
1	**cup chopped ripe olives**
¾	**cup shredded Cheddar cheese**
1	**cup seasoned Italian breadcrumbs**
2	**teaspoons salt**
1	**teaspoon pepper**
1	**teaspoon cayenne pepper**
1	**teaspoon dried oregano**
1	**Tablespoon butter**
	Garnish: Paprika
1	**Tablespoon minced parsley**

Parboil eggplant 20 minutes or until tender. Cool. Halve and scoop out the pulp leaving the shells intact. Mash the pulp and add peppers, onions, olives, cheese, breadcrumbs, salt, pepper, cayenne and oregano. Reserve a small amount of cheese and breadcrumbs. Refill the shells. Dot with butter. Top with reserved cheese and crumbs. Sprinkle with paprika and parsley. Bake at 325 degrees 30 minutes.

This may also be baked without the shell in a greased casserole and will serve 4.

CABBAGE ROLL CASSEROLE

Perfect for your January suppers!

1	**large head green cabbage**
1	**pound ground venison, beef or lamb**
½	**cup chopped onion**
2	**garlic cloves, minced**
½	**cup chopped parsley**
	Salt and pepper to taste
¼	**teaspoon cinnamon**
1	**cup cooked rice**
2	**10-ounce cans diced tomatoes with green chilies**

In a large pot bring about ½ cup seasoned water to a boil. Put cabbage in and cook until tender, do not over cook. In a skillet brown meat, seasoning with onion, garlic, parsley, salt, pepper and cinnamon. Drain well! Drain most of the water off the cabbage and return to pot. Top cabbage with meat, rice and tomatoes. Cover and simmer about 15 minutes. Check seasonings.

Serve with cornbread. Don't forget the Tabasco!

ASPARAGUS CASSEROLE

4　12-ounce cans whole asparagus, drained, reserving juice
4　hard-cooked eggs, sliced
1　cup chopped celery
2　teaspoons grated onion
4　Tablespoons butter
¼　cup all-purpose flour
½　cup asparagus juice
1½ cups whole milk or half-and-half, warmed
1　teaspoon Worcestershire sauce
½　teaspoon cayenne pepper
1　cup shredded Cheddar cheese
½　cup sherry
1　cup crushed Ritz crackers

Layer asparagus and chopped eggs in a big casserole dish. Sauté celery and onions in butter add flour, blending in well and slowly add warm milk and asparagus juice to make sauce. Add Worcestershire sauce, pepper, cheese and sherry, blend well. Pour over asparagus. Check seasonings, may need to add a little salt. Top with about 1 cup crushed Ritz crackers. When ready to serve, bake a 350 degrees about 30 minutes or until hot and bubbly

ASPARAGUS TIPS

1 **bunch firm asparagus with compact tips**

Refrigerate stalks upright in a container of cold water. Or wrap the bottom of the stalks in a damp towel, seal in a plastic bag and refrigerate. Use within four days. Just before cooking, cut off about two inches from the bottom of each stalk and rinse well. May steam stalks 5 to 6 minutes or cook in boiling salted water 3 to 4 minutes. Serve immediately or submerge in cold water. May saute and stir fry later.

Asparagus is low in fat and sodium and rich in vitamins A and C, niacin, calcium, potassium and phosphorus. For all that, one cup cooked chopped asparagus contains about 40 calories.

GREEN BEAN CASSEROLE

This is the good one!

This is like fried chicken, everybody likes it. Great for a covered dish occasion! Perfect to take for the funeral lunch, a vegetable comfort food, and this dish will be gone. Don't you just hate to take something to an occasion and yours is still left? I know there are some purist cooks that turn their noses up at mushroom soup...but it sure is good sometimes!

2	Tablespoons butter, melted
1	large onion, chopped
1	large garlic clove, chopped
2	15-ounce cans whole green beans, drained and rinsed in cold water
1	teaspoon cayenne pepper
½	teaspoon salt
1	10¾-ounce can cream of mushroom soup
1	cup whole or evaporated milk
1	8-ounce package shredded sharp Cheddar cheese or processed cheese spread
1	can French fried onions

In your black iron skillet, melt butter and sauté onion and garlic until limp. Add green beans and toss gently. Cook about 5 more minutes. Add red pepper and salt. Set aside. In a sauce pan, heat soup, milk and cheese, stirring until cheese melts. Add the beans, be careful and try not to break them up. Gently fold in about ½ cup of the French fried onions. Check seasonings. Pour into a buttered baking dish. Bake in a 350 degree oven about 25 minutes or until hot and bubbly. Sprinkle about 1 cup of the onions on top and bake 5 or 10 minutes more.

GREEN BEANS, MARINATED

Wonderful and easy. A makeahead, because it just gets better and better!

⅓   **cup sugar**
⅓   **cup olive oil**
½   **cup white wine vinegar**
2   **Tablespoons soy sauce**
2   **Tablespoons Worcestershire sauce**
½   **teaspoon pepper**
½   **teaspoon paprika**
1   **jar pimento**
3   **to 4 green onions, tops and bottoms, chopped**
1   **clove garlic, pressed**
1   **small bell pepper, chopped**
4   **cans whole green beans, drained and rinsed**

Mix first 11 ingredients and pour over beans. Refrigerate overnight. Serve in a pretty glass bowl lined with red tip lettuce.

These green beans are just perfect for a BRUNCH. Serve along with SAUSAGE BREAKFAST CASSEROLE (pg. 71), HOT CURRIED FRUIT, CHEESE GRITS (pg. 98), and SOUR CREAM BISCUITS (pg. 80) with different jellies and preserves, such as figs.

Pass an assortment of wonderful little pick-up DESSERTS or an easy delicious POUND CAKE. Serve this with fresh fruit and whipped cream.

TOASTED PECANS are nice to have, placed around your entertaining area in little bowls. I always like to have some on the bar.

SPINACH MADELEINE

Need we say more?

When I think of a good spinach, I think of SOPHIA BLANKS! She has some of the best parties around and the best food, too!

2   10-ounce packages frozen chopped spinach, thawed
4   Tablespoons butter
2   Tablespoons all-purpose flour
½   cup spinach liquor
½   cup evaporated milk
½   cup chopped onion
½   teaspoon pepper
¾   teaspoon celery salt
¾   teaspoon garlic salt
    Salt to taste
1   6-ounce roll garlic cheese, cut into small pieces
1   teaspoon Worcestershire sauce
    Cayenne pepper to taste

Cook spinach according to directions. Drain and reserve liquor. Melt butter in saucepan over low heat, Add flour, stirring until blended and smooth, but not brown, Add liquid slowly, stirring to avoid lumps. Cook until smooth and thick; continue stirring. Add seasonings and cheese, which has been cut into small pieces. Stir until melted. Combine with spinach. Check seasonings, you may need a little more salt or red pepper.

I always add juice of a lemon and some of the zest to my spinach, might try it, its good!

This may be served immediately or put into a casserole, topped with buttered bread crumbs. This freezes well and doubles easily.

They say this serves 5 or 6, but it is so good, I say it serves about 4.

TOMATO DRESSING

Wonderful with baked chicken or a good grilled steak and oh so pretty on your plate!

1   **stick butter**
1   **large onion, coarsely chopped**
4   **stalks celery, coarsely chopped**
3   **garlic cloves, minced**
½   **cup chopped parsley**
4   **cups chopped tomatoes drained, reserving juice**
2   **bread slices, soaked in tomato juice then juice squeezed out**
1   **teaspoon sugar**
    Salt and pepper to taste
¼   **teaspoon ground allspice**
¼   **teaspoon ground nutmeg**
¼   **teaspoon curry powder**
    Garnish: Chopped parsley

Melt butter in a sauce pan and sauté the onions, celery, garlic and parsley until limp. Add drained tomatoes. Stir in squeezed bread, mixing well. You do not want clumps of the bread. Add seasonings and check. Pour in a buttered baking dish, sprinkle with dry parsley and bake in a preheated 350 degree oven for about 30 minutes or until hot and bubbly.

ARTICHOKE ITALIA

You are going to be surprised how good and easy this is!

This is JESSICA INABNETT's grandmother's recipe. She and her husband, CARRICK, served this savory casserole for a dinner party in their lovely home. Carrick's pork tenderloin was not bad either. Mike and I had so much fun. Their children, MARY SNELLINGS, CARRICK Jr., and baby BREARD, are just darling and very entertaining! I have always said it is more trouble to have a few friends over for dinner than having 100 for cocktails!

1	16-ounce can French cut green beans, drained
1	14-ounce can artichokes, drained and quartered
½	cup grated Parmesan cheese
¾	cup Italian breadcrumbs
3	green onions, chopped
2	large garlic cloves, chopped
½	cup olive oil
½	teaspoon cracked red pepper, optional
1	thinly sliced lemon, optional

Mix all together. Bake in a lightly greased Pyrex dish, at 350 degrees, for about 30 minutes.

WHITE BEANS AND ITALIAN SAUSAGE

1   **pound dry white beans**
8   **to 10 cups cold water**
1   **Tablespoon ham base or ham flavored bouillon**
1   **onion, chopped**
2   **garlic cloves, chopped**
½   **cup chopped celery**
½   **cup chopped parsley**
1   **to 2 hot peppers**
1   **large bay leaf**
    Salt and pepper to taste
2   **cups 1-inch round carrots**
1   **pound Italian sausage**
2   **cups finely chopped green onions, tops and bottoms**
    French bread or cornbread

Rinse and sort beans. Soak over night. Next day, drain, cover with cold water, add the next 7 ingredients and bring to a boil. Reduce heat and cook about 2 hours or until beans are very tender. Add salt and pepper. Add carrots. Cut sausage into ½-inch rounds. Fry over low heat in skillet until slightly browned. Drain sausage on paper towels and add to bean mixture. Continue cooking slowly for about 45 more minutes. Check seasonings. Serve in big bowls and garnish with green onions. Serve with a hot crusty French bread or hot cornbread. A big green salad would be nice.

You could use lamb shanks instead of the sausage and it is wonderful!

CHEESE GRITS CASSEROLE

SARA DESHOTEL, our daughter, LESLEY`S wife, MARY VIRGINIA AND THOMAS`s mother, makes these best. She serves this with a nice HONEY BAKED HAM, GREEN BEAN HORSERADISH, BAKED APPLES and SOUR CREAM BISCUITS, with FIG PRESERVES! Now that is good!

NIEMAN MARCUS BROWNIES are perfect for that little something SWEET!

3   10½-ounce cans chicken broth
½   cup whipping cream
1   teaspoon salt
1   cup grits
4   Tablespoons butter
1   8-ounce package shredded sharp Cheddar cheese
½   teaspoon cayenne pepper
    Garnish: Paprika and dried parsley

In a large saucepan, combine broth, cream and salt, bring to a boil. Gradually stir in grits. Reduce heat to low; cover and cook about 5 minutes, stirring occasional. You may need to add a little more water. Remove from heat. Add cheese and butter; stir until melted. Add red pepper and check salt. Mix well. Pour mixture into a greased casserole and bake at 350 degrees until hot and bubbly. Sprinkle with paprika and dry parsley. Let stand about 10 minutes before serving.

Green Beans Horseradish, page 168, Fig Preserves, page 153, Neiman Marcus Brownies, page 295, are in Cooking and Gardening with Dianne, my first book.

Variation You can add 1 teaspoon garlic powder or cooked sausage or ham. Sometimes I like to add about ½ cup chopped jalapeños, especially if I am serving them with game. SO GOOD!

DIRTY RICE

My children's favorite! I love to use fresh wild duck gizzards. When making this , I usually boil enough duck gizzards to have plenty to fry for dinner. They are so good. You almost want to throw the duck away and keep the gizzards! Not really, but they are that good. The duck gizzards are really hard to clean but well worth the extra effort. Most hunters throw them away. Shame on you, you are missing the best part!

1   pound gizzards and hearts (wild fowl, chicken or turkey)
½   pound pork sausage or good Italian sausage
1   large onion, chopped
1   small bell pepper, chopped
1   cup chopped celery
2   garlic cloves, minced
2½ cups dry rice, cooked in reserved liquid
1   stick butter
2   10¾-ounce cans cream of mushroom soup
1   cup chopped green onions, tops and bottoms
½   cup chopped parsley
½   teaspoon dried thyme
    Salt, pepper and cayenne to taste

Boil gizzards and hearts in salted water until very tender. Drain and reserve cooking liquid. Finely chop gizzards and hearts. May chop in the food processor. Bump them 2 or 3 times, but not too much! Cook sausage over low heat until lightly browned. Add onions, peppers, celery and garlic. Simmer, stirring occasionally until vegetables are tender. Add cooked rice, butter, soup, chopped meat, green onions, parsley, thyme, salt, pepper and cayenne. Gently stir mixture. If possible add meat drippings. Pour mixture into a 13 x 9 x 2-inch baking dish. Cover with foil and bake at 350 degrees 45 minutes.

Better prepared a day in advance. Dish freezes well also.

(Dirty Rice, continued)

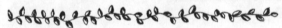

I served this for Christmas with a turducken
(a boneless chicken stuffed into a boneless duck, stuffed
into a boneless turkey, except for exterior wings and truncated
drumsticks (a word you can look up in Mr. Webster). Each
bird is stuffed with a delicious dressing, which holds it together.
Besides being easy to slice and a beautiful presentation, it
is absolutely wonderful and really easy to cook. I made a
light gravy with the drippings and served it along with
the dirty rice. An explosion of flavors!

Perfect for a big holiday celebration! Feeds 20 to 25 people.
Hebert's of Maurice, Louisiana, invented this specialty.
There are several locations you can order from. They also
have wonderful boneless chickens, stuffed crawfish,
shrimp or cornbread dressing, ready for the oven.
Get on the computer!

CORN PUDDING

Corn Pudding is the "Company" dish.

4 **Tablespoons butter**	Melt butter in a saucepan.
¼ **cup all-purpose flour**	Whisk in flour, salt and
2 **teaspoons salt**	sugar. Cook and stir until
1½ **Tablespoons sugar**	bubbly. Slowly add milk
1¾ **cups milk**	and cook until thickened.
3 **cups fresh or frozen**	Stir in corn and eggs. Pour
corn, chopped	mixture into a well buttered
3 **eggs, beaten until**	3-quart casserole dish.
frothy	Bake in a hot water bath at
	350 degrees 45 minutes.

CORN FRITTERS

When DAVID VITTER, our US Senator, was in the KNOE Studios, we fixed "Fritters for Vitter."

4   ears corn
1   egg, beaten
1   teaspoon sugar
¼   cup all-purpose flour
2   teaspoons baking
     powder
     Salt, pepper and
       cayenne pepper to
       taste
1   teaspoon bacon
     drippings, optional
1   to 2 Tablespoons
     chopped peppers,
     optional
     Vegetable shortening
       for frying

Cut corn from cob. Mix with egg and rest of ingredients to make a thick batter. Drop each teaspoon full into hot grease and fry till nice and golden brown. Drain on lots of paper towel. Serve immediately! May want to sprinkle with a little salt.

CHILI-LIME CORN ON THE COB

SHERMAN SHAW has the sweetest corn of all! NEIL MOTT too!

4   ears corn, shucked
½   cup light sour cream
4   teaspoons finely chopped fresh cilantro
2   teaspoons chili powder
1   teaspoon fresh lime juice
    Salt and pepper to taste
2   Tablespoons butter

Cover corn with plastic wrap on a microwave-safe platter and microwave on high until corn is fully cooked (8-10 minutes).

Mix sour cream, cilantro, chili powder, lime juice, salt and pepper, cover and chill unitl ready to serve.

Just before serving the corn, heat butter in a 12-inch skillet over medium-high heat. Add corn and cook, turning with tongs every few minutes. Cook until it turns golden brown.

Serve immediately with sour cream spread on the side.

This is so fast and so easy! Use your microwave to cook the corn, and you can save so much time!

CHOUX GLORIFIED

You almost think you are eating asparagus!

1   large cabbage,
    chopped
2   onions, chopped
3   garlic cloves, minced
    Vegetable oil
1   stick butter
2   bread slices, soaked
    in milk to moisten
    well
1   pint heavy cream or
    half-and-half
5   slices shredded
    American cheese
    Salt and cayenne
    pepper to taste
    Italian breadcrumbs

Parboil cabbage in salted water. Drain thoroughly and set aside. Saute onions and garlic in oil until tender. Add cabbage to onions. Add butter, moistened bread, cream and cheese. Stir well. Sprinkle with salt and cayenne. Pour half mixture into an 11 x 7 x 2-inch casserole dish. Top with half breadcrumbs. Cover with remaining cabbage mixture and sprinkle with breadcrumbs. Bake at 350 degrees 30 minutes or until browned.

ROASTED SWEET ONIONS

4   medium sweet onions
2   Tablespoons
     Worcestershire
     sauce
4   Tablespoons butter
     Salt, pepper and
     cayenne pepper to
     taste

Remove tops and skin of onions. Cut an X halfway through each onion. Brush with Worcestershire sauce. Dot with butter and sprinkle with salt, pepper and cayenne. Wrap each onion in heavy-duty foil and seal. Place over hot coals and roast, turning occasionally, 45 to 50 minutes or until tender.

Foil wrapped onion may be oven roasted at 350 degrees, for about an hour or until tender, or cover with plastic wrap and microwave about four minutes. May also cover with plastic wrap and microwave about 4 minutes.

SCALLOPED CELERY

4 cups coarsely
    chopped celery
¼ cup blanched slivered
    almonds
1 6-ounce can water
    chestnuts, chopped
1 4-ounce can
    mushroom stems
    and pieces, drained
1 10¾-ounce can
    cream of chicken
    soup
1 cup chicken broth
1 Tablespoon
    cornstarch
    Salt and pepper to
    taste
½ cup dry breadcrumbs
½ cup Parmesan cheese

Boil celery in salted boiling water 5 minutes. Drain. Combine celery, almonds, water chestnuts and mushrooms. Set aside. In a saucepan, combine soup and broth. Bring to boil. Reduce heat and simmer 5 minutes. Whisk in cornstarch. Add salt and pepper. Pour mixture into a greased 2-quart casserole dish. Combine breadcrumbs and cheese. Sprinkle on top. Dot with butter. Bake at 375 degrees 20 to 25 minutes or until hot and bubbly.

It is best to make this ahead of time and refrigerate at least 24 hours before baking.

MACARONI AND CHEESE

Macaroni and cheese has made a big come back. All I hear lately is MACARONI AND CHEESE. There are all kinds of ways to prepare this great American dish. You can put your own twist to this dish from ham to peppers, mushrooms, different cheeses, white sauces to cottage cheese. They are all good but I think this is the very best, the old fashion way! This is the one before HARRY WEISHAAR who worked for KRAFT FOODS back in the 1940's came up with macaroni and cheese in a box. This is the one our Grandmothers made!

2	cups dry macaroni
1	stick, butter
2½	cups, shredded sharp Cheddar cheese
4	eggs
2	cups milk
1	can, evaporated milk
	Salt and black pepper to taste
	Pinch of ground nutmeg
	Buttered breadcrumbs (optional)
	Garnish: paprika

Boil macaroni until *al dente* – almost done! Pour a layer of macaroni into a greased 1½ quart casserole. Top with layer of cheese and butter. Repeat layers, as this will insure that your macaroni and cheese is juicy!

Beat eggs and mix with milk and seasonings. Pour over macaroni. Bake in a 350 degree oven, loosely covered with foil, about 30-45 minutes or until almost set. Let stand or rest about 15 minutes before serving. Do not overbake. As it sets, it will tighten up.

This recipe easily doubles or triples.

Macaroni and cheese as an American classic first appeared in Fannie Farmer's cookbook in 1896, which listed baked macaroni with Parmesan cheese and a topping of browned breadcrumbs.

BAKED POTATO COWBOY CASSEROLE

This was served at the informal rehearsal dinner for Jerry Wolff and Colette Crain in Dallas at Sammy's Bar B Que. Sammy's is a trendy spot for the in the know Dallas crowd. The wedding took place at the magnificent Presbyterian Church in Highland Park with the reception following at the Dallas Country Club. Not one stone was left unturned, from the bride to the flowers, food and music, it was just beautiful.

I could not get these potatoes off my mind! This is just a big old baked potato, ready to go and so easy to serve!

6   **to 8 normal baking size Russet potatoes**
1   **stick butter**
   Salt and pepper
1   **16-ounce carton sour cream**
   Sharp Cheddar cheese, medium sliced

Scrub potatoes with your little potato brush. Pat dry, spray with Pam or rub with a little bacon drippings. Sprinkle or roll in a little Tony's or Cavender's and wrap each potato in foil. Bake in a 350 degree oven about an hour and half or until done. Unwrap potatoes and place in a big baking dish. Slice length wise, sort of crushing in, put lots of butter, salt, pepper and sour cream. Cut the dressed potato across in about 3 or 4 pieces, keeping the potato together. You may want to add a little more butter and sour cream and more salt and pepper. Randomly add slices of the Cheddar cheese. Cover with foil. When ready to serve heat in a 350 degree oven about 30 minutes.

(Baked Potato Cowboy Casserole, continued)

These are even better the next day. This is so simple, so easy and so good. You could add chopped green chilies or finely chopped green onions.

Crispy fried bacon would be good to sprinkle on the top when ready to serve.

The NATIONAL POTATO COUNCIL says not to store POTATOES in the ice box. The STARCH in the potatoes changes to SUGARS in the fridge and this makes the potatoes have a sweet taste. The best place for potatoes is a cool dark pantry or a storage location with good air circulation. NEVER use plastic bags, only paper bags or open bins.

SUMMER PASTA

3   to 4 tomatoes, chopped
1   cup chopped basil
3   cups shredded mozzarella cheese
     Grated Parmesan cheese
⅓   to ½ cup olive oil
3   garlic cloves, minced
     Salt and pepper to taste
     Red pepper
1   pound pasta of your choice, cooked al dente

Combine tomatoes, basil, mozzarella cheese, Parmesan cheese, oil and garlic. Refrigerate 3 to 4 hours. Add salt, pepper and pasta. Toss to coat.

May add cooked shrimp or chicken. Good hot or cold. Also may add chopped green onions, black olives or capers.

OKRA JAMBALYA

Fresh okra is one of my most favorite vegetables. You can fry it, smother it, stew it and you cannot mess it up! Try trimming the okra, gently boiling it until just tender. Drain, while hot, and pour over a good French dressing. Refrigerate it and serve it cold in salads or as little hors d'oeurve! Mmmmm!

The name gumbo is derived from Guingombo, a West African word meaning OKRA!

4	or 5 dozen fresh, tender young okra, trimmed
½	stick butter or 2 Tablespoons bacon drippings
1	medium onion, chopped
2	cloves garlic, minced
1	small bell pepper, minced
½	cup parsley, minced
1	cup green onions, tops and bottoms, finely chopped
3	cups tomatoes, chopped, or 1 can Rotel (optional)
1	cup sausage or ham, sauteed(optional)
2	teaspoons salt
1	teaspoon black pepper
½	teaspoon cayenne pepper
	Tabasco Sauce
1	cup long-grain rice
2	cups well-seasoned chicken stock

In a Dutch oven, melt butter or drippings; saute onion, garlic and pepper 6 to 8 minutes. Add tomatoes, parsley, okra and seasonings. Cook about 20 minutes, until tender. Cook rice in stock and toss in okra mixture. Serve immediately or reheat in a Pyrex dish covered with foil.

Serve with a nice green salad and hot French bread, with lots of creamy sweet butter. This is also a wonderful side dish.

Wild Game
&
Meats

JACK MINER'S TESTIMONY

The Father of
North American Conservation

The Lord is my Guide and Teacher, I will not get lost;
He makes my heart a receiving station for His wireless;
He sits down beside me in the pathless woods and opens
up His book of knowledge; He turns the leaves very slowly that
my dimmed eyes may read His meaning.

He makes the trees I plant to grow, and flowers to arch
my path with their fragrant beauty; gives me dominion over
the fowls of the air and they honk and sing their way
to and from my home.

Yea, He has brought me up from a barefooted
underprivileged boy to a man respected by millions of
people, and I give Him all the credit and praise whenever,
wherever, and forever.
~Jack Miner

Jack Miner is considered the father of conservation on
the North American continent. A market waterfowl hunter
around the turn of the 20th Century, Miner one February
afternoon in 1904 transformed himself from a killer of waterfowl to their most ardent protector.

The deeply religious Miner, who died in 1944 at the age of
79, formed the Jack Miner Waterfowl Sanctuary in 1904
with this statement:

"I've been their enemy. I wonder if they will have me for a friend?"

The Jack Miner Waterfowl Sanctuary tags each bird with a
band containing the contact information of the sanctuary
as well as a bible verse, continuing Jack Miner's tradition of
ministry and conservation. One such band, embossed with
1st Peter 5:7, "He careth for you," was returned with the
following apology: "I'm sorry, but I've just killed your first
pet."

Miner has left behind a name and a legacy that will live forever in the thoughts of everyone who is a believer and advocate of the conservation of wildlife. The sanctuary is open to the public in Kingsville, Ontario, Canada.

DUCK WRAPS

That Mallard Farm Way! MIKE CAGE, JR. does these best. You cannot make enough of these. Do plenty because you are going to run out!

Duck breast, cut into 1 to 1½-inch strips
Smoke marinade
Favorite jelly
Worcestershire sauce to taste
Jalapeño peppers, cut into narrow strips
Cream cheese, sliced
Thin bacon slices, halved
Toothpicks

Cut the duck breast in 1-inch to 1½-inch strips, lightly flatten out. Marinade in sauce that you have prepared. Layer in breast, jalapeño and cheese, roll up and wrap in a half piece of bacon, secure with a toothpick. Grill over hot coals about 5 to 7 minutes. Do not over cook! You want this pink in the middle.

When cooking venison or ducks, as there is not a lot of fat, you need to quick cook it or cook it a long time, slowly.

FRIED DUCK GIZZARDS

You are in for a real treat! This will make you want to throw the duck away and keep the gizzards! They are tough to clean, but oh what a treat!

**Duck Gizzards, well
  cleaned
Celery
Onions
Garlic
Bell pepper
Bay leaf
Hot pepper
Buttermilk
Self-rising flour
Salt and pepper
Paprika
Fresh peanut oil**

To clean your duck gizzards, remove all fat from outside. Split the gizzards from the opening side and peel out course membrane until inside is glistening white. These freeze well, until ready to use.

Using a dutch oven, season water very well with all the good stuff (peppers, onions, garlic). Add gizzards and bring to a boil. Reduce heat and cook for 4 to 5 hours until gizzards are fork-tender. Drain and save your stock for Dirty Rice or gravy.

To fry, soak in buttermilk and shake in well-seasoned flour. Fry in hot, fresh peanut oil for 2 or 3 minutes or until a nice, light brown. Sprinkle with salt and serve immediately with a jezabel sauce or a marchant de vin.

WILD ITALIAN DUCK FETTUCCINE

4   whole wild ducks
    Bay leaf
1   onion, chopped
    Chopped celery
    Salt and pepper to
      taste
½   cup olive oil
½   cup all-purpose flour
1   large onion, chopped
1   large bell pepper,
    chopped
4-5 garlic cloves,
    chopped
1   cup milk
3   to 4 cups duck broth,
    which you have
    defatted
1   cup chopped green
    onions
½   cup chopped parsley
1   6-ounce can pitted
    black olives
    Cayenne pepper,
    dried oregano and
    ground thyme to
    taste
½   cup chopped basil or
    2 tablespoons dried
1   12-ounce package
    spinach fettuccine,
    cooked al dente
    Parmesan cheese

Cover ducks with water. Add bay leaf, onions, celery, salt and pepper. Bring to boil. Reduce heat and simmer until tender, about 2 hours. Remove meat from bone and cut into bite size pieces. Set aside. In a cast iron skillet, heat oil. Whisk in flour, to make a light roux. Add onions, peppers and garlic. Cook until tender. Slowly add milk and broth, stirring to make a thin gravy. Add green onions, parsley, olives, meat, salt, pepper, cayenne, oregano, thyme and basil. Remove bay leaf. Mix with cooked pasta. Pour mixture into a shallow baking dish. Cover and bake at 350 degrees about 20 minutes. Make sure dish has enough liquid. Sprinkle with cheese and bake an additional 10 minutes. Serve with hot garlic bread and a good green crisp salad.

Some breast their ducks. When you cook the whole bird, you get more flavor for most dishes!

ORANGE SAUCE FOR DUCK

2 cups fresh orange juice
4 Tablespoons minced green onions
3 Tablespoons white wine vinegar
2 Tablespoons dry white wine
   Packed brown sugar
10 Tablespoons chilled unsalted butter
2 2¾-inch wide strips orange peel, cut julienne
   Salt, pepper and ground nutmeg to taste

Combine juice, green onions, vinegar, wine and brown sugar in a heavy saucepan. Simmer, stirring until sugar dissolves. Bring to boil. Cook and stir 25 minutes or until sauce is reduced by half. Remove from heat. Whisk in 4 pieces chilled butter. Return to low heat. Whisk in remaining 6 pieces butter, one piece at a time. Remove pan from heat if drops of melted butter appear. If sauce breaks, remove and whisk in two Tablespoons of chilled butter. Stir in orange peel. Add salt, pepper and nutmeg. Spoon over carved roasted duck.

For this sauce,
I recommend Duck
La Louisiana (Cooking
& Gardening, pg. 201).
It is perfect with
this sauce!

FRIED QUAIL

There are many fancy ways of cooking quail but this is hard to beat.

Quail
Buttermilk
Well seasoned
    all-purpose flour
    with paprika
Peanut oil

Soak quail in buttermilk. Dredge in flour. Deep fry in hot oil. If frying whole, fry 10 to 12 minutes or until golden brown. (Half a bird, cook 8 minutes.) Do not overcook.

No one cooks these better than

Velynda Clifton Shaw. Birds or any game should not be kept over one year. Enjoy while it is nice and fresh.

SKEWERED & GRILLED DOVE BREASTS

Birds, remove breasts
Bacon slices, halved
Toothpicks
Italian dressing

Wrap breasts in bacon half. Skewer several breasts. Marinade in dressing. Grill, basting with marinade, over hot coals 5 to 20 minutes. Do not overcook. I like my doves a little on the rare side. Serve with jalapeño cheese grits, green bean bundles and hot curry fruit with lots of hot French bread.

VENISON, THAT FRIED CHICKEN WAY!

Like eating candy! Fry plenty, because with all those tasters, it is hard to have enough for dinner! Great for big cocktail parties!

Venison chunks, about silver dollar size
2 eggs, beaten
1 cup water
Seasoned flour
Salt, pepper and paprika to taste
Peanut oil

Pound venison out as thin as you can. Beat eggs and mix with water. Dip venison in egg mixture and then in seasoned flour. Deep fry in hot fresh oil about 2 minutes or until light brown. Do not over cook, you want to quick fry it. Keep the oil hot but try not to burn it!

Serve with hot biscuits and cream gravy, purple hull peas, fresh tomatoes, and slices of purple onion!

This goes quite well with cream gravy and rice, too!

CREAM GRAVY

2 Tablespoons flour
2 cups light cream or
 milk
½ teaspoon salt
½ teaspoon white
 pepper

When finished frying venison, spoon off all but 2 Tablespoons of fat from skillet, leaving brown bits in the pan for added flavor. Whisk in flour until smooth. Cook over medium heat, stirring, for 1 minute. Gradually whisk in cream or milk, stirring constantly, until mixture comes to a boil. Season to taste with salt and pepper. Serve in a gravy boat or serving bowl.

Variation: For frying, instead of the egg-water mixture, buttermilk is really good. You have more crust and it's more flakey.

CROWN OF PORK

DELIA and HOODIE Allen of Morehead, Kentucky do this best! What a way to welcome a houseguest. One of the most beautiful and fun dinner parties I have ever been to and it was for me. I love you Delia!

Crown of pork,
16-18 ribs
1 cup apple cider
Salt and pepper to
taste
Cooked peas and
carrots or cooked
wild or white rice
Chopped parsley or
watercress
Crab apples

Have your butcher shape your pork ribs into a crown. Place in a shallow roasting pan. Insert meat thermometer into center of meaty part on one chop. Season with salt and pepper. Roast at 325 degrees about 3 hours or until thermometer reaches 185 degrees. Baste with cider and pan juices. To serve, place crown on a serving platter. Fill the center with peas and carrots or rice topped with parsley. Surround with crab apples.

If you are ambitious, the last 30 to 45 minutes, Delia filled the center with a corn soufflé. Surround roast with spiced peaches or peach halves filled with chutney. Makes a delicious accompaniment to roast pork.

GRILLED PORK TENDERLOIN STUFFED IN TORTILLAS WITH A RASPBERRY JALAPEÑO SAUCE

John and Alpha Spence know how to throw a party. Their food is wonderful and they share their beautiful home with all!

2	pork or beef tenderloins
	Olive oil
	Worcestershire sauce to taste
	Salt and lemon pepper to taste
1	11½-ounce package flour tortillas, 8-inch size
1½	cups raspberry preserves, or strawberry or Mayhaw
½	cup finely chopped jalapeño peppers
¼	cup finely chopped cilantro
1	teaspoon salt
⅛	teaspoon ground cumin
	Garnish: Chopped parsley

Marinate tenderloins in oil, Worcestershire sauce, salt and lemon pepper. Grill or cook in a hot skillet with a little oil about 5 to 6 minutes on both sides until tender. Do not overcook. Slice thin and sprinkle with salt. Cut 3 circles with a 3-inch cookie cutter from each tortilla. Warm circles in a large skillet with a little butter or olive oil and set aside. Combine preserves, peppers, cilantro, salt and cumin in a saucepan. Bring to a slow boil. Remove from heat. Dip tenderloin slices in sauce. Place one meat slice on warm tortilla and fold over. Arrange on a platter, close together. Garnish with parsley.

Beautiful on your buffet and a real crowd pleaser. May be served warm or at room temperature. May also prepare ahead.

GRILLADES AND GRITS

2	large onions, coarsely chopped
4	bell peppers, coarsely chopped
½	cup coarsely chopped celery
4	garlic cloves, finely chopped
½	cup finely chopped parsley
2	bay leaves
½	cup vegetable shortening
1	6-ounce can tomato paste
4	cups water or beef broth
2	Tablespoons cornstarch
3	Tablespoons water
1	Tablespoon dried thyme
	Salt, pepper and cayenne pepper to taste
6	veal or venison steaks, 4-ounces each
	All-purpose flour
1	Tablespoon bacon drippings
1	recipe Grits Soufflé (Cooking & Gardening, pg. 83)

Saute onions, peppers, celery, garlic, parsley and bay leaves in hot shortening 5 to 10 minutes. Add tomato paste and beef broth. Simmer 20 minutes. Dissolve cornstarch in water. Gradually add to vegetable mixture. Add thyme, salt, pepper and cayenne. Simmer until mixture thickens. Remove from heat. Remove bay leaves. Season steaks with salt and pepper. Dredge in flour. Saute in drippings until browned. Arrange steaks in 13 x 9 x 2-inch baking dish. Cover with sauce. Bake at 350 degrees 30 minutes or until tender. Serve with Grits Soufflé.

I do not like to serve my grillades with Cheese Grits.

LAMB CHOPS

This is from MARIE LOUISE SNELLINGS "Cook": "I like lamb chops a tiny bit rare as opposed to a leg of lamb."

    Bacon drippings
    Kitchen Bouquet
4   Lamb chops
¼   cup water
1   teaspoon
      Worcestershire
      sauce
2   Tablespoons butter

Heat bacon drippings in a hot iron skillet. Rub chops with Kitchen Bouquet and throw in skillet. Brown quickly. Before they have a chance to stick, turn chops over. Reduce heat and cook 2 to 3 minutes, depending upon thickness of chops. Transfer to a warm platter. Add water to skillet. Scrape bits from bottom of skillet. Add Worcestershire sauce and butter. Cook and stir to make a gravy. Pour gravy over chops and serve.

Another nice way to make chops, is to fry in butter in a skillet with canned sliced pineapple. Use 1 slice pineapple with each chop. Cook pineapple until browned. Place chops in center on platter with pineapple arranged on outside.

MEAT CONCERN

A good "do ahead" for a larger crowd!

1	15-ounce can cream-style corn
1	15-ounce can tomatoes
	Salt to taste
2	Tablespoons butter
¼	cup chopped onions
¼	cup finely chopped bell peppers
½	cup sliced mushrooms
1	Tablespoon butter
½	cup chopped celery
1½	pounds ground beef
2	hot peppers, chopped
1	10¾-ounce can tomato soup
	Worcestershire sauce and pepper to taste
1	package vermicelli, cooked al dente
	Shredded cheese of your choice

Combine corn, tomatoes, salt and butter in a stockpot. Cook 5 minutes. Set aside. Saute onions, peppers and mushrooms in butter until tender. Add celery, beef and peppers. Cook until meat is browned. Add to corn mixture. Stir in Worcestershire sauce, pepper and cooked pasta. Simmer 30 minutes. If possible refrigerate overnight. One hour before serving, pour mixture into a buttered 13 x 9 x 2-inch baking dish. Dot generously with butter and sprinkle with cheese.

Bake at 325 degrees 1 hour. This freezes well.

SOUTHWEST SCENTED TENDERLOIN

Tenderloins:

3   Tablespoons paprika
3   teaspoons ground
       cumin
1   Tablespoon cilantro
2   Tablespoons pepper
1   teaspoon ground
       nutmeg
1   teaspoon cayenne
       pepper
1   Tablespoon salt
       Beef or pork
       tenderloins

Tenderloin: Two to three days before serving, combine paprika, cumin, cilantro, pepper, nutmeg, cayenne and salt. Rub seasonings into tenderloin. Wrap in foil and refrigerate. Grill over hot heat about 8 minutes. Baste with sauce once or twice. Let sit 3 minutes before cutting. Serve with remaining sauce.

Sauce:

1½ sticks butter
       Zest of 2 limes
       Juice of 2 limes
¼   cup chopped cilantro
       Salt and pepper to
          taste

Sauce: Melt butter in a saucepan. Add zest, juice, cilantro, salt and pepper. Baste meat while grilling.

THE SPAGHETTI GARDEN ITALIAN SPAGHETTI SAUCE AND MEATBALLS

When we were children, Mama used to send one of us, out of the four, down Park Avenue to the Spaghetti Garden with her big black iron Dutch oven. For $4.00 Mrs. Lasuzzo would fill it up with the best spaghetti and meatballs I have ever had. This recipe is close.

1   **onion, chopped**
3   **to 4 garlic cloves, minced**
2   **Tablespoons olive oil**
2   **8-ounce cans tomato sauce**
2   **6-ounce cans tomato paste**
4   **cups water**
1   **teaspoon dried oregano**
⅛   **teaspoon chili powder**
2   **teaspoons sugar**
½   **teaspoon dried basil**
1   **teaspoon salt**
1   **teaspoon pepper**

Saute onions and garlic in oil. Add tomato sauce and paste. Bring to boil, stirring well. Reduce heat and simmer 30 minutes. Add water, oregano, chili powder, sugar, basil, salt and pepper. Simmer 3 hours. May add more water. For meatballs, you may make your own but the frozen ones are really good and so easy. The sauce is the best part of the recipe.

I like to crumble Italian sausage and cook it slowly, drain off the fat well, then add to sauce. You want mostly sauce and small amount of meat. Serve over spaghetti pasta with garlic bread and a good cold green salad. A full-bodied red wine is nice with this.

STUFFED BELL PEPPERS

Peppers, peppers, peppers! Red, green, yellow and orange, so pretty. Put them in a big wooden bowl on your kitchen counter and enjoy for several days before cooking. You get two for one, an arrangement and a wonderful dinner. Perfect for any occasion.

6   bell peppers
1   pound ground chuck
    or turkey
½   pound sausage or
    venison
1   small onion, chopped
1   cup finely chopped
    green onions, tops
    and bottoms
1   to 2 garlic cloves,
    minced
½   cup chopped celery
2   Tablespoons butter or
    olive oil
1   slice white bread,
    moistened and
    squeezed
1   cup cooked rice
3   eggs, slightly beaten
    Salt, pepper and
    cayenne pepper to
    taste
½   cup breadcrumbs
    Paprika and dried
    parsley to taste

Cut the peppers in half, carefully removing the seeds. Boil about 5 minutes and drain.

Brown meat in skillet and drain off any fat. Sauté onions, garlic and celery in butter or oil and add to meat mixture. Shred moistened bread and work into meat mixture. Add seasonings and eggs. Mix well and check seasonings.

Stuff meat in peppers. Sprinkle with bread crumbs, paprika and a little dry parsley. Bake in a 350 degree oven for about 30 minutes. Serve with hot French bread and a nice ice cold green salad with good tomatoes and a little oil and vinegar.

You can make these two or three days ahead, cover and refrigerate until ready to bake.

Variation: Use shrimp or crawfish seasoned with lemon juice instead of the meat.

COTTAGE PIE (SHEPHERD'S PIE)

Typical English Pub Fare and oh so good on those cold damp days. A good way to use that leftover roast, steak, pork, lamb or ground beef. You can add a little leftover ham or diced link sausage.

3	Tablespoons vegetable oil
3	Tablespoons all-purpose flour
1	onion, chopped
½	cup chopped celery
1	bell pepper, chopped
3	to 4 garlic cloves, minced
½	cup chopped parsley
1	cup finely chopped carrots
3	to 4 cups leftover meat, chopped
2	to 3 cups hot broth, may use bouillon
	Salt and pepper and herbs de Provence
1	to 2 Tablespoons Kitchen Bouquet
4	to 5 medium potatoes
4	Tablespoons butter
½	cup hot milk

Heat oil in a large skillet. Whisk in flour until browned. Saute onions, celery, peppers, garlic, parsley and carrots until tender. Add meat and slowly add hot broth, stirring well. Add lots of salt, pepper and herbs de Provence. Simmer 45 minutes. May need to add more broth. Add Kitchen bouquet. You want a nice juicy gravy not too thick but not too thin.

Boil potatoes in salted water until tender. Drain and mash potatoes. Add butter and milk and whip until smooth. Add salt and pepper. Spread potatoes in the bottom of a 13 x 9 x 2-inch baking dish. Push potatoes up the side of dish, making a well in the center. Pour meat mixture over potatoes. Bake at 350 degrees 30 to 35 minutes or until gravy bubbles around the edge. Serve with green peas. This may be made in advance and refrigerated.

(Cottage Pie [Shepherd's Pie], continued)

While touring in Scotland, we stopped in a wonderful pub in St. Andrews. This was served in individual salad plate size Yorkshire pudding shells. So good and pretty to serve.

CHEESEBURGER PASTA

This is a specialty at Semolinas in Shreveport. They serve it just on Thursdays and it is always a sell out, so get there early.

Tagliati or bowtie pasta
Processed cheese loaf, cubed
Seasoned hamburger patties, cooked and broken up
Grilled onions
Shredded lettuce
Tomatoes, coarsely chopped or cherry tomatoes, halved
Dill pickles
Shoestring potatoes
Mustard
BBQ sauce, optional
Salt and pepper to taste

Cook pasta according to package directions. Drain leaving a little cooking water. Add cheese cubes and toss. To assemble, spoon pasta on individual plates. Top with hamburger pieces, onions, lettuce, tomatoes, pickles, shoestring potatoes and mustard. Add salt and pepper. Enjoy!

This is so easy and would be fun for a party. Maybe on Monday night football, let everyone fix there own cheeseburger pasta. Have big platters or bowls of the above.

STUMP, BUBBLE, AND SQUEAK

Typical European Fare in England, Belgium, Ireland, France and Germany.

Bratwurst
Sausage
Pork Chops
Red potatoes
Milk, butter, salt and
   pepper to taste
Onions and garlic,
   sauteed in butter or
   olive oil
Sauerkraut
Carrots, steamed

Slowly pan fry bratwurst, sausage and chops until done. Boil potatoes until tender, drain and mash, adding milk, butter, salt and pepper. Spoon potatoes into a 13 x 9 x 2-inch baking dish. Bake at 350 degrees 30 minutes. Place meat on a serving platter. Top with onions and garlic. Arrange sauerkraut and carrots on platter. Serve with baked mashed potatoes and cornbread.

Seafoods

OYSTERS CARIBBEAN

This is a delicious Creole dish!

1   **quart oysters, drained, save the liquid**
2   **Tablespoons bacon drippings**
1   **Tablespoon butter**
3   **Tablespoons flour**
1   **onion, finely chopped**
1   **bell pepper, finely chopped**
1   **hot pepper**
3   **cloves garlic, minced**
½   **cup parsley, finely chopped**
1   **cup green onions, tops and bottoms, finely chopped**
1   **Tablespoon Pernod**
     Salt, pepper and red pepper to taste
1   **Tablespoon lemon juice and some of the zest**
     Paprika
1   **Tablespoon Kitchen Bouquet**

In a large black iron skillet add drippings and butter and heat until hot, add flour and make a dark roux. Add onion, peppers, garlic and cook until limp. Add oysters, parsley and green onions, gently stirring. Add seasonings. If mixture is too thick, thin with a little oyster liquor. Be careful, the oysters will make liquid and you want this not too thin but not too thick. You want it just right, like nice thin gravy. Check seasonings. This should be a dark chocolate brown; you may need to add more Kitchen Bouquet.

Serve in a shallow soup bowl with hot garlic bread or with rice. This is also wonderful served in Pepperidge Farm patty shells but do put in shells until ready to serve.

OYSTER CASSEROLE

A favorite of the DESHOTEL Family!

3   dozen oysters
1   cup chopped parsley
1   cup chopped green
    onions
1   cup rolled cracker
    crumbs
1   stick butter, melted
1   lemon, sliced
½   teaspoon dry mustard
2   teaspoons
    Worcestershire
    sauce

Drain oysters and place in a shallow baking dish. Sprinkle with parsley and onions. Top with crumbs. Pour butter over all. Top with lemon slices. Combine mustard and Worcestershire sauce. Drizzle over oysters. Bake at 450 degrees 10 to 15 minutes.

CRABCAKES

That Summer Southern Way!

ELEANOR BROWN passed these, before dinner, at one of her fabulous parties. It set the tone for a delightful evening! BILLY BROWN, who is one of the smartest lawyers in Louisiana, several years ago, was approached to run for Governor. He said no, but if he did, the best thing for Louisiana would be having Eleanor as our first lady.

1	**stick butter**
¼	**cup finely chopped onions**
¼	**cup finely chopped celery**
¼	**cup finely chopped parsley**
½	**cup finely chopped green onions, tops and bottoms**
2	**garlic cloves, finely minced**
¾	**cup breadcrumbs**
¼	**teaspoon dried thyme**
1	**teaspoon pepper**
1	**teaspoon salt**
½	**teaspoon cayenne pepper**
	Zest of 1 lemon
1	**tablespoon lemon juice**
1	**egg, beaten**
2	**tablespoons mayonnaise**
1	**tablespoon prepared mustard**
1	**pound lump crabmeat, shells removed**

Melt butter in a large skillet. Saute onions, celery, parsley, green onions and garlic. Fold in breadcrumbs. Add thyme, pepper, salt, cayenne, zest and juice. Stir in egg, mayonnaise and mustard. Mix well and taste for flavor. Gently fold in crabmeat. Shape mixture into desired size patties. Place on a foil lined baking sheet. Cover with wax paper and refrigerate. For oven baking, spray foil with cooking spray. Dot each cake with butter. Bake at 400 degrees 20 minutes. To pan fry, melt butter or oil until hot in a large skillet. Fry cakes 1½ minutes on each side until lightly browned. Serve with a good tartar sauce.

May make miniature patties and pass at big cocktail parties!

STUFFED CRÊPES FOR TWELVE

Perfect for a Ladies' Luncheon!

Filling:

1	stick butter
½	cup minced green onion
2	pounds lump crabmeat, checked for shells
	Salt and pepper to taste
	Dash of garlic powder, optional
½	cup vermouth

Melt butter in a large skillet. Saute onions. Add crabmeat and cook 3 minutes. Stir in salt, pepper and garlic powder. Add vermouth and bring to boil. Boil until liquid is evaporated. Scrape filling into a bowl and set aside.

Sauce:

⅔	cup vermouth
¼	cup cornstarch
¼	cup milk
4	cups heavy cream
	Salt and pepper to taste
2½	cups shredded Swiss cheese or more to taste
	Butter

In same skillet, add vermouth. Bring to boil and reduce to 2 tablespoons. Remove from heat. Whisk together cornstarch and milk. Add to skillet. Return to heat. Slowly add cream. Stir in salt and pepper. Cook 5 minutes until thickened. Add 1½ cups cheese. Cook until cheese melts. Mix well.

Preparation: *Prepare 24 crêpes using crêpe recipe from Cooking and Gardening with Dianne. To assemble, blend half sauce with crabmeat filling. Place a large spoonful of filling on each crêpe. Roll up and place seam side down in a buttered 13 x 9 x 2-inch baking dish. This recipe will fill two baking dishes. Repeat with filling and remaining crêpes. Spoon sauce over crêpes and sprinkle with remaining cheese. Dot with butter. Refrigerate. Remove from refrigerator 30 minutes before baking. Bake at 400 degrees 20 minutes or until hot and bubbly. Serve with a little tossed salad and a little white wine. A dining pleasure. This dish may be frozen.*

This recipe is Marilyn Irby's and it is perfection!

SHRIMP AND GRITS

BRAVE NEW SHRIMP are a must for this low country dish! Brave New Shrimp are farm raised in beautiful Southern Arkansas. Handled with kid gloves and TLC, they arrive fresh from the crystal clear water of the Deep South right to your kitchen. Order online at www. bravenewshrimp.com.

Grits:

1½ cups grits
4   cups seasoned
      chicken broth
4   tablespoons butter
1   tablespoon chopped
      parsley
      Salt to taste

Grits: Cook grits according to package directions using chicken broth instead of water. Stir occasionally to keep from sticking. When thick, add butter, parsley and salt. Pour into a greased casserole dish. When ready to serve, bake at 350 degrees about 30 minutes or until hot and bubbly.

Shrimp:

4   tablespoons butter
½   cup olive oil
1   large onion, chopped
1   medium bell pepper,
      chopped
1   small sweet red
      pepper, chopped
1   cup chopped celery
2   garlic cloves,
      chopped
½   cup chopped parsley
1   cup chopped green
      onions, tops and
      bottoms
4   cups hot well
      seasoned chicken
      broth

Shrimp: Heat butter and oil in a large Dutch oven. Saute onions, bell peppers, sweet peppers, celery, garlic, parsley and green onions until tender. Slowly add hot broth, stirring well. Add tomatoes. Stir in cornstarch mixture. Add saffron, paprika, lemon pepper, salt, pepper, cayenne, thyme and bay leaf. Stir well. Cover and simmer 30 minutes, stirring occasionally. Test for flavor. Do not want mixture

(Shrimp and Grits, continued)

1   16-ounce can
      chopped tomatoes
½   cup cornstarch,
      dissolved in 1 cup
      broth
    Pinch of saffron
    Paprika to taste
1   teaspoon lemon
      pepper
    Salt, pepper and
      cayenne pepper to
      taste
½   teaspoon ground
      thyme
1   bay leaf
1½ pounds shrimp,
      peeled and
      deveined

to be too thick. Add shrimp and simmer an additional 10 minutes. Remove from heat. Let stand for flavors to blend. Remove bay leaf. Serve over cooked grits with hot crusty French bread and sweet creamy butter. A big ice cold green salad is just perfect with the yummy dish.

Shrimp mixture is best the day in advance for flavors to really blend. Try adding 1 cup chopped Andouille sausage in the sauce for a different flavor that is delightful. Course grind yellow grits are good, if you can find them. Low Country cooking at its best.

SHRIMP KABOBS

Whether at the beach or at their beautiful home on Bayou DeSiard, LAURA and JESSE WIED have mastered this! Just ask MARY AMANDA, KATHERINE, and HANNAH. The secret is good fresh shrimp.

3-4 pounds of 8 to 10 count shrimp, peeled and deveined
Pineapple chunks, reserving juice
Sweet red or bell peppers, cut into bite size pieces
Onions, cut into bite size pieces
Italian salad dressing
Cooked rice
2 tablespoons butter, melted
Salt and pepper to taste

Marinate shrimp, pineapple, peppers and onions in dressing for 2 hours. Skewer shrimp and vegetables. Reserving dressing. Cook over medium heat coals or just until shrimp turn pink. Do not overcook. Serve as an appetizer or main course over rice. Combine dressing, pineapple juice, butter, salt and pepper in a small skillet. Cook and stir until reduced by half. Pour sauce over kabobs. Serve with a green salad and hot French bread.

SALMON...GRILLED OR BROILED

If any is left, this makes a good niçoise salad or salmon salad!

2 or 3 pound salmon filet
½ cup butter
½ cup parsley, chopped
½ cup green onions, finely chopped
Old Bays Seasonings or Tony's Lemon pepper
Juice of 1 lemon and the zest
1 lemon thinly sliced
Parsley, finely chopped

Preheat oven to 450 degrees or have coals medium hot. Make a heavy foil boat, sides turned up, like a shallow baking dish. If you are cooking on the grill, place fish in foil boat directly over the coals, if in oven, place on a baking sheet. Brush with melted butter and season with onions, parsley, Old Bays, lemon pepper and lemon juice and zest. Bake in oven about 20 to 25 minutes or on the grill about the same time. Do not over cook! I like my salmon more on the rare side. Spoon drippings over and garnish with lemon slices and chopped parsley.

Remember that fish, when removed from the heat, will continue to cook, so you must be very careful not to over cook!

GROUPER

Our family's favorite saltwater fish. We like to cook this when the GROUPER was swimming the day before!

If you have any left over, perfect for a GROUPER BURGER! Fix it just like a good old hamburger but use a tartare sauce instead of mayo and mustard.

6 **Grouper filets**
½ **stick butter**
1 **Tablespoon olive oil**
   Old Bay seasoning
   Paprika
½ **cup flour**
1 **lemon, juiced and the zest**
½ **cup parsley, finely chopped**
½ **cup green onions, finely chopped**
½ **cup white wine**

In a large black iron skillet heat butter and oil. Season filets with Old Bay and paprika, lightly dredge in flour. In the hot skillet sauté filets 2 minutes, turn add lemon, parsley and green onions, cook 2 more minutes. Remove fish to a warm platter. In the piping hot skillet add wine and reduce the sauce, pour over fish, garnish with parsley and serve immediately!

If you are doing this for a large seated dinner, say 12 guest, using the directions above, (except for reducing the sauce), line a baking sheet with foil and cook filets in a preheated 450 degree oven for about 8 minutes, garnish with extra butter and parsley.

Once for a large cocktail party I cooked 30 filets in the oven, placed them on a

(Grouper, continued)

big glass platter, garnished with parsley, lemon slices and placed a bowl of tartare sauce or the Lemon Anchovy Dressing in the middle of the platter and served with homemade toast points. A beautiful presentation and a big hit! It is easy too. Serve at room temperature or this is good cold!

CRAWFISH PIE

What a rich pie! LYNN BRYANT makes this best! Just ask BUNZY!

1	**pound crawfish tails**
4	**tablespoons butter**
1	**bunch green onions, chopped**
½	**cup chopped parsley**
4	**tablespoons butter**
3	**tablespoons all-purpose flour**
1	**pint half-and-half**
3	**tablespoons sherry**
1	**tablespoon lemon juice**
1	**tablespoon lemon zest**
	Salt, pepper and cayenne pepper to taste
1	**9-inch pie shell, baked**

Saute crawfish in butter 10 minutes. In a separate skillet, saute onions and parsley in butter. Whisk in flour. Add half-and-half, stirring constantly until thickened. Add sherry, juice and zest. Stir in crawfish. Add salt, pepper and cayenne. Pour mixture in pie shell. Bake at 350 degrees 20 minutes. Freezes well.

SALMON CROQUETTES

ANN WILSON shared this recipe. It's so good and so easy!

Salmon:

2   7½-ounce cans pink salmon or the vacuum pack
½   cup finely chopped onions
½   cup finely chopped celery
1   teaspoon dried tarragon
    Salt and pepper to taste
½   cup mayonnaise
1   tablespoon Dijon mustard
1   egg, slightly beaten
1   cup crushed cracker crumbs
    Crushed cracker crumbs
    Olive oil
    Melted butter
    Garnish: Lemon slices and parsley sprigs
1   cup carrots, grated
1   cup cabbage, grated or slaw mix

Combine salmon, onions, celery, tarragon, salt, pepper, mayonnaise, mustard, egg and 1 cup cracker crumbs. Mix well. Shape mixture into patties. Roll in cracker crumbs. Refrigerate at least 1 hour. Heat oil and butter in a large skillet. Pan fry patties until golden brown. Toss shredded carrots and cabbage with a little tartar sauce or Rémoulade sauce. Serve salmon over bed of carrots and cabbage. Garnish with lemon slices and sprigs of parsley.

Your favorite slaw would be good with this dish!

(Salmon Croquets, continued)

Rémoulade Sauce:

Mayonnaise
Creole mustard
Finely chopped green
   onions, tops and
   bottoms
Chopped parsley
Capers
Horseradish sauce
Lemon juice
Paprika
Salt and pepper to
   taste

Whip together mayonnaise, mustard, onions, parsley, capers, horseradish sauce, juice, paprika, salt and pepper until smooth. Taste for desired flavor.

CREOLE BAKED CATFISH

2   cups fish fry or good
    cream meal
2   teaspoons salt
1   teaspoon pepper
1   teaspoon cayenne
    pepper
1   teaspoon lemon
    pepper
8   3 to 4-ounce catfish
    filets
1   teaspoon Creole
    seasoning
4   tablespoons butter,
    melted
½   cup finely chopped
    parsley
    Garnish: Lemon
    wedges

Combine cornmeal, salt, pepper, cayenne and lemon pepper. Dredge filets in mixture. Place skin side down on a greased baking sheet. Sprinkle with Creole seasoning. Drizzle with butter. Bake at 400 degrees 30 minutes or until golden and fish flakes easily. Sprinkle with parsley. Garnish with lemon wedges.

A SAUTE OF FRESH FISH FILETS WITH GARDEN VEGETABLES AND PASTA

Seasoned salt
½ cup all-purpose flour
Olive oil
Eggplant, sliced
Tomato, chopped
Bell pepper, chopped
Hot pepper, chopped
Green onions,
  chopped, optional
Chopped parsley,
  optional
8 filets, perch, bream
  or bass
Pasta of choice,
  cooked al dente and
  keep warm
Chopped garlic

Saute eggplant, tomato, bell pepper, hot pepper, green onions and parsley in oil until tender. Remove from skillet and set aside. Sprinkle fish with salt and quickly saute in oil. Mound pasta in the middle of a warmed platter. Place fish around platter and top with vegetables. Sprinkle a little flour in the hot skillet and cook until lightly browned. Add a few peppers, garlic and a little pasta water. Cook and stir sauce until reduced. Pour sauce over fish.

Serve with a nice crispy green salad and cold Chardonnay. Light the candles! Enjoy.

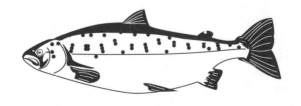

HOT TUNA SANDWICHES

A VIRGINIA WARNER Special!

Tuna Sandwiches:

½ 4-ounce can chopped
    mushrooms
1   7-ounce can white
    tuna fish
1   10¾-ounce can
    cream of mushroom
    soup
4   hard-cooked eggs,
    chopped
1   4½-ounce can ripe
    olives, chopped
2   tablespoons
    mayonnaise
½   teaspoon onion salt
    Butter and melted
    butter
    White sandwich bread

Combine mushrooms, tuna, soup, eggs, olives, mayonnaise and onion salt. Butter bread slices. Spread tuna mixture over butter. Stack bread to make triple-decker sandwiches. Wrap in wax paper. Refrigerate at least 1 hour. Brush each sandwich with melted butter. Place on baking sheet. Bake at 350 degrees 25 minutes.

Sauce:

2   cups white sauce
1   10¾-ounce can
    cream of mushroom
    soup
1   4-ounce can chopped
    mushrooms
    Shredded Cheddar
    cheese

Combine white sauce, soup and mushrooms. Heat, stirring constantly. Top sandwiches with sauce and sprinkle with cheese. Serve sandwiches hot with cold marinated green beans.

SHRIMP OR CRAWFISH ENCHILADAS

1 **pound small shrimp or crawfish**
2 **tablespoons olive oil**
1 **cup chopped bell pepper**
1 **cup chopped sweet red pepper**
1 **small onion, chopped**
1 **cup chopped tomatoes, drained**
1 **to 2 jalapeño peppers, chopped**
2 **garlic cloves, minced**
1 **tablespoon dried oregano**
1 **teaspoon salt**
1 **teaspoon cayenne pepper**
½ **teaspoon pepper**
1 **cup evaporated low fat milk**
1 **10¾-ounce can cream of shrimp soup**
1 **cup light sour cream**
1 **cup shredded sharp Cheddar cheese**
1 **cup shredded Monterey Jack cheese**
Cayenne pepper and salt to taste
Large flour burrito size tortillas
1 **bunch green onions, chopped**

Saute shrimp in oil with half of each of peppers, onions, tomatoes and garlic. Add oregano, salt, cayenne and pepper. Cook until vegetables are tender. Set aside. In a saucepan, combine milk, soup, sour cream and both cheeses. Cook and stir until cheese melts. Add cayenne and salt. Place a large dollop of shrimp mixture in tortilla. Roll up and place seam side down in a 2-quart baking dish. If there is leftover filling, just add to sauce. Pour sauce on top. Sprinkle with green onions. Cover and bake at 350 degrees 30 to 40 minutes or until hot and bubbly. Remove foil and bake uncovered 10 minutes. Serve with Calypso Black Bean and Corn Salad.

Variation: You can do the same recipe and use a 2 to 3 pound chicken, cooked, boned and cubed. Mix in a can of chopped green chilies, little ground cumin and chili powder. Always season well and use lots of onions, garlic and peppers. It makes such a difference.

COURTBOULLION

For fresh fish, shrimp, or crawfish.

4 cups fish filets, cut up, bream, white perch or bass
Lemon pepper or lemon juice
2 large onions, chopped
2 bell peppers, chopped
1 sweet red pepper, chopped
1 bunch green onions, chopped, tops and bottoms
2 to 3 garlic cloves, chopped
4 to 5 stalks celery, chopped
2 tablespoons olive oil
4 cups stewed tomatoes or half stewed and half tomatoes with green chilies
Cayenne pepper, paprika, dried oregano and ground cumin to taste
Worcestershire sauce and dried parsley to taste
1 tablespoon packed brown sugar
Hot cooked rice or pasta

Marinate fish in lemon pepper or lemon juice overnight. In a large stockpot, Saute onions, peppers, green onions, garlic and celery in oil until tender. Add tomatoes. Stir in cayenne, paprika, oregano, cumin, Worcestershire sauce, parsley and brown sugar. Simmer 10 minutes. Add fish pieces and gently stir. Cook 3 to 4 minutes. Serve over pasta or rice with a nice crispy green salad and hot crusty French bread.

SUMMERTIME GUMBO

We are going to use the roux in a jar! So much easier and I promise just as good!

Remember a good GUMBO in not supposed to be a thick stew or gravy like mixture! The thickness of your Gumbo depends on the amount of water or a wonderful seasoned stock! There are all kinds of variations; this is one of my favorite's. In the spring and summer everything is in season and so fresh for this wonderful gumbo!

4	heaping Tablespoons Savoie's roux
4	quarts water or a well seasoned stock
1	large onion, chopped
1	large bell pepper, chopped
1½	cups celery, chopped
3	cloves garlic, chopped
1	package gumbo crabs, 1 to 2 pounds sack
1	pound link sausage, coarsely chopped, cook and drain fat
1	cup green onions, tops and bottoms, chopped
1	cup fresh parsley, chopped
1½	pounds okra, stewed with 1 cup chopped tomatoes
2	pounds, medium, shrimp
2	or 3 bay leaves Salt, pepper, red pepper and Old Bay Kitchen Bouquet

Dissolve roux in water over medium heat and let boil gently for ½ hour. Add the next 6 ingredients and cook over low heat for ½ hour. Add the rest of the ingredients and simmer another 30 minutes. If you need a little more color, add a little Kitchen Bouquet, you can get any color you want! Check seasonings. If something is missing it is usually salt!

Serve over of hot fluffy rice with crusty French bread with a good, ice cold green salad.

The River Road Cookbook of Baton Rouge says this best; Gumbo is a wonderful means of using leftovers; bits of ham or a ham bone, turkey, duck or chicken carcass, sausage, seafood's

(*Summertime Gumbo, continued*)

or bacon. When using a carcass or hambone, boil the bones and use the stock in the gumbo. You can freeze the stock for later use.

I have been making Gumbo for the last 40 years and I have never seen or heard of a BROKEN ROUX!

HOW TO BREAK A ROUX: When making a roux, always add cold (as vegetables) to your hot roux to cool it off. If you add hot broth instead, the roux will break and it can not be saved. Conversely if you let it cool completely, then you can add hot broth. You say, how will I know if I broke my roux, trust me you will know! It is the biggest curdled mess you have ever seen. The fat and stock will not blend. Just throw it out and start over or better yet use a good commercial roux!

NOTES

Desserts

AMARETTO ICE CREAM SANDWICH DESSERT

Oh Oh Oh...Good, Good, Good, Good....Easy, Easy!

Our daughter, SARA CAGE DESHOTEL, wife of LESLEY ARMOND DESHOTEL, I love that name, and mother of VIRGINIA and THOMAS, served this at one of our big family Sunday suppers. It was a big hit with young and old. Plan on taking a nice long walk after this decadent dessert. Very easy and for those who are not in the know, think it is glorious.

1   **box ice cream sandwiches**
1   **cup Amaretto**
1   **8-ounce jar caramel topping**
3   **to 4 toffee candy bars, crushed reserving ½ cup**
1   **16-ounce container frozen whipped topping, thawed**
     Pecans, lightly toasted and chopped

Layer ice cream sandwiches in a 13 x 9 x 2-inch baking dish. Pierce holes in sandwiches with a handle of a wooden spoon. Drizzle Amaretto over all. Cover with caramel topping. Sprinkle with crushed candy. Spread topping over all. Top with remaining candy and nuts. Freeze. Cut into squares. Serve on a pretty crystal dessert plate, garnish with a little flower or sprig of mint.

SWEET POTATO ICE CREAM

6   eggs, separated
2⅓ cups sugar
1   13-ounce can
      evaporated milk
2   14-ounce cans
      sweetened
      condensed milk
1½ tablespoons vanilla
3   cups cooked,
      creamed sweet
      potatoes, drained
8   cups homogenized
      milk

Beat egg whites until stiff. Add egg yolks, sugar, evaporated milk, condensed milk, vanilla, sweet potatoes and milk, beating well after each addition. Freeze in a hand or electric freezer.

ALMOND MACAROON ICE CREAM DESSERT

Be sure to use a good ice cream, such as Premium. MIKE CAGE spells Premium DYNAMITE!

3   dozen almond
      macaroons
1   cup whiskey
      Toasted almonds
2   quarts Premium
      vanilla ice cream,
      softened

Soak macaroons in whiskey. Line a glass bowl with wax paper. Place a layer of almonds in bottom. Spread 1 quart ice cream on top. Spread remaining macaroons on top. Spoon on second quart of ice cream. Garnish with a fresh mint or pretty little flower, like a pansy.

This is so easy and pretty to serve. This is also a good make-ahead dessert.

PUMPKIN ROLL

Fun to make in the fall! I got this recipe from my good friend, DEBBIE CLICK, who got it from her mother, JOHNNIE NEALY. Johnnie is a wonderful cook.

Roll:

1 **cup sugar**	
¾ **cup all-purpose flour**	
1 **teaspoon baking soda**	
1 **teaspoon salt**	
1 **teaspoon cinnamon**	
3 **eggs**	
¾ **cup canned pumpkin**	
Powdered sugar	

Combine sugar, flour, baking soda, salt and cinnamon. Stir in eggs and pumpkin. Mix well. Pour mixture into a greased jelly-roll sheet. Bake at 350 degrees 10 minutes. Place roll on a tea towel that has been sprinkled with powdered sugar. Roll up with towel and let cool.

Filling:

2 **tablespoons butter, softened**
1 **8-ounce package cream cheese, softened**
1 **teaspoon vanilla**
1 **cup powdered sugar**

Cream butter, cream cheese and vanilla. Add powdered sugar. Blend until creamy. Gently unroll roll and spread with filling. Roll up and refrigerate. Slice when ready to serve.

WHITE TRASH

This is a darling Christmas gift and real cute in red containers, like a red bucket. You can mix different cereals, like rice or wheat or whatever. Enjoy!

Everyone loves a celebrity! Monroe-West Monroe's very own GREG JORDAN, the international decorator, several years ago gave all his high falooting friends and clients, from New York to Paris to California, this for Christmas! Greg passed away this April. What a sad loss for his family and so many friends. He will be missed.

1	**20-ounce almond bark coating or good white chocolate**
1	**10-ounce package oat cereal**
1	**12-ounce package corn chex cereal**
1	**15-ounce package stick pretzels**
2	**cups peanuts**
2	**cups pecans**

Melt coating, stirring until smooth. Combine cereal, pretzels and nuts. Drizzle with coating, tossing gently. Toss until almost dry. Break into small pieces

"Quality of life is what really matters. It's about keeping your eye on what connects everybody, of realizing that we all basically want the same things – comfort, security, to be loved. I try really hard to never lose sight of that."

Greg Jordan
1956-2005

FALLEN CHOCOLATE CAKE

First time we had this was in Reims, France. I fell in love with the cake and made Mike take me back to LE VIGRNO the next night. Chef Andrea came over to the table and I oohed and aahed over the cake. The chef was really good looking! Mike Cage, I think, got a little jealous. Under his breath he muttered, "I would like to see that so and so take out a kidney." I said, "Well if he did or could, I'll bet he could cook it!" At this point, we were on our second bottle of VEUVE CLIQUOT!

1 **8-ounce package semi-sweet chocolate squares**
1 **stick unsalted butter**
4 **large eggs**
1 **egg yolk**
1 **teaspoon vanilla**
¼ **teaspoon salt**
½ **cup sugar**
2 **tablespoons all-purpose flour**
   Garnish: Ice cream or whipped topping

Melt chocolate in a microwave, about 2 minutes. Add butter and microwave about 1 more minute. Whisk together and set aside. In a separate bowl, beat eggs, egg yolk, vanilla, salt and sugar. Beat at high speed until it triples in volume and is light in color. Pour egg mixture over chocolate mixture. Sprinkle with flour. Fold in well. Pour mixture into buttered and floured ramekins. May refrigerate at this point until ready to bake. Bring back to room temperature before baking. Bake at 400 degrees 12 to 13 minutes. Invert cakes onto dessert plates. Serve with ice cream or whipped topping and maybe raspberries or strawberries.

I always love to garnish with a fresh sprig of mint or a pretty garden flower.

KAY'S FAMOUS CHOCOLATE CAKE

God has blessed me, more than once. I had three garden weddings, without a backup plan and the weather was glorious each time! You can imagine all the hustle and bustle going around the house the week of the occasions. Sweet KAY DIXON walks in with her famous cake for all to enjoy!

Cake:

2 cups sugar
2 sticks butter, softened
2 eggs
¾ cup cocoa powder
½ teaspoon salt
1 teaspoon vanilla
1 cup buttermilk
1 teaspoon baking soda
2½ cups all-purpose sifted flour
1 cup boiling water

Cream sugar, butter and eggs. Blend in cocoa, salt and vanilla. In a separate bowl, mix together buttermilk and baking soda. Add milk and flour alternately to creamed mixture. Mix until smooth. Stir in hot water. Batter will be thin. Grease and line two 9-inch round cake pans with wax paper. Evenly pour mixture into prepared pans. Bake at 350 degrees 35 minutes. May also bake in a jellyroll pan for 20 to 25 minutes.

Icing:

1 stick butter
3 tablespoons cocoa powder
6 tablespoons milk
5 cups powdered sugar
1 tablespoon vanilla

Combine butter, cocoa and milk in a saucepan. Bring to boil. Remove from heat. Add vanilla and powdered sugar. Use more powdered sugar for a thicker icing. Mix well. Frost cake with icing.

TRES LECHES (THREE MILK CAKE)

This was served for my 58th birthday party in CABO SAN LUCAS, MEXICO. I am so lucky! We celebrated December birthdays with our good friends CAROL and BOB CUDD, CONNIE and NAT TROY, ANNIE and BILL BROWN and ANN and BERT KAPLAN. Talk about a fun, easy group! It was also Carol's and Bill's birthday and with all being on different days, we celebrated on each big day. To tell the truth, we celebrated everyday! This cake was just for me. So wonderful, I had to find the recipe. This is the good one!

Cake:

10 **egg yolks, room temperature for 30 minutes**
½ **cup sugar**
1 **tablespoon vanilla**
10 **egg whites**
½ **cup sugar**
1 **cup all-purpose flour, sifted**
1 **tablespoon baking powder**
   Powdered sugar

Beat egg yolks 20 minutes until light and lemon colored. Should be very thick. Add sugar, 2 tablespoons at a time. Add vanilla and beat 3 minutes. Transfer to a large bowl. Wash mixing bowl well. Whip egg whites until soft peaks form. Add sugar. Beat until stiff. Fold the whites into the yolk mixture one third at a time. Add flour and baking powder all at once. Mix well. Pour batter into a well greased 10½-inch springform pan. Bake at 350 degrees 45 to 60 minutes or until cake pulls away from sides. Let stand 5 minutes. Run a knife around the edge of cake. Remove sides of pan. Dust with powdered sugar. Place cake on a serving plate with a slight dip.

(Tres Leches [Three Milk Cake], continued)

Glaze:

¾ **cup sweetened condensed milk**
½ **cup heavy cream**
1 **cup evaporated milk**
2 **tablespoons rum, brandy, mezcal or liquor of choice**

Combine condensed milk, cream and evaporated milk. Add liquor. Pierce holes in the cake with a skewer. Slowly pour small amount of glaze over cake. Allow soaking in before pouring more. Cover and refrigerate.

Variation: This is wonderful with fresh strawberries or raspberries. A little scoop of vanilla ice cream on the side is nice but the cake stands on its own. You can make this like a jelly-roll with filling and frosting if you wish.

SWISS LEMON CUSTARD PUDDING CAKE

This dessert will have custard on the bottom and sponge cake on top. Wonderful and so easy.

6   tablespoons all-purpose flour
6   tablespoons butter, melted
1½ cups sugar
4   egg yolks
1½ cups milk
     Zest of 1 lemon
2   tablespoons lemon juice
4   egg whites
½   cup sugar
     Powdered sugar

Combine flour, butter and sugar. Beat egg yolks. Add to flour mixture. Stir in milk, zest and juice. In another bowl, beat egg whites until stiff. Gradually beat in sugar. Fold egg white mixture into batter. Pour batter into a greased 2-quart baking dish or individual ramekins. Place in a shallow pan of water. Bake at 350 degrees 55 minutes or until lightly browned. Dust with powdered sugar. Serve warm or cold.

May serve with fresh strawberries or raspberries and a sprig of mint. Pansies are also a pretty decoration.

FRIENDSHIP CAKE

That vanilla wafer way! CAROLYN LEPPICH makes this cake for Christmas presents for her special friends. She collects old, pretty plates from estate sales, garage sales, antique sales and such. What a perfect gift. A fabulous cake on a beautiful old plate! A gift from the heart!

2   **sticks butter, softened**
2   **cups sugar**
6   **eggs**
1   **12-ounce box vanilla wafers, crushed**
½   **cup milk**
1   **7-ounce package flaked coconut**
1   **cup pecans, chopped**

Cream butter and sugar. Add eggs, one at a time, beating well after each addition. Add crushed wafers and milk. Mix in coconut and pecans. Pour batter into a very well greased tube pan. Bake at 275 degrees 2 hours or until done. Cool 30 minutes before inverting onto a serving plate. Carolyn's comes out perfect. I have trouble!

Before opening wafers, cut several slits in bag and crush wafers with a rolling pin.

This cake is very hard to get out of the tube pan. May try lining with a piece of parchment paper. Even though it might fall apart, it is wonderful.

CARAMEL FLAN CAKE

What a show-off! This is one big, rich cake!

1   12-ounce jar caramel
    topping
1   18-ounce package
    yellow cake mix or
    chocolate mix
1   8-ounce package
    cream cheese,
    softened
5   large eggs
1   12-ounce can
    evaporated milk
1   14-ounce can
    sweetened
    condensed milk
1   cup whole milk
1   teaspoon vanilla
Garnish:
    Strawberries,
    raspberries,
    blackberries or kiwi

Pour topping in bottom of a 12-cup Bundt pan. Prepare cake according to package directions. Pour batter over topping. Blend cream cheese and eggs in a blender. Slowly add evaporated milk, condensed milk and whole milk. Add vanilla and blend until smooth. Pour mixture over batter. Cover tightly with foil. Place Bundt pan in a 2 to 3-inch water bath. Bake at 350 degrees 1 hour, 30 minutes. Remove from water bath and cool 15 to 30 minutes. Invert cake on a big pretty plate with a rim. Cool and refrigerate until ready to serve. Garnish with berries, kiwi, pansy or mint.

This cake is rich so the berries are a must and really compliment the cake. This is so easy and the burst of flavor is amazing.

Be sure you have the right equipment. You may have a little too much milk for the Bundt pan. Be sure to leave a space of about 1½ inches from the top so the batter will not run or bake out. It might all fit in fine. I think bake for only 1 hour, 30 minutes and let cool. It does not get as firm. Just a thought! Try pineapple cake mix and pineapple topping!

THE WEDDING CAKE

*This is the one you dream about! The very best!
CAROLE KILPATRICK shared this one with me. Her
husband Tex reminds me of Andy Griffith.*

Cake:

1 18-ounce package
   white cake mix
1 teaspoon almond
   extract
2 tablespoons Amaretto

Prepare cake according to package directions except use ice water. Add extract and Amaretto. Pour batter into 2 round cake pans. Bake according to package directions.

Glaze:

1 cup water
1 cup sugar
1 teaspoon almond
   extract
1 tablespoon Amaretto

Bring water and sugar to boil. Reduce heat and cook until slightly thickened. Add extract and Amaretto. Cool. Drizzle glaze over cooled cake layers, allowing soaking in before adding more.

Butter Cream Icing:

1 cup vegetable
   shortening
2 16-ounce packages
   powdered sugar
1 teaspoon almond
   extract
1 tablespoon Amaretto
¼ teaspoon salt

Cream shortening and powdered sugar. Add extract, Amaretto and salt. Frost cake layers.

SHIRLEY BROWN'S POUND CAKE

You think you are eating homemade pound cake. Wonderful and so easy! SHIRLEY served this with fresh strawberries. She sliced strawberries, covered with sugar and little water. Cover strawberries and refrigerate several hours. The berries were spooned over each slice of cake with a dollop of real whipped cream. You can go anywhere and you will not find anything better!

1 **18-ounce package yellow cake mix** 4 **eggs** ½ **Crisco oil** 1 **8-ounce container sour cream** 1 **teaspoon vanilla** 1 **teaspoon almond extract**	Combine all ingredients and beat for 1 minute. Scrape sides of bowl and beat for 1 minute. Pour into a bundt pan that has been sprayed with Pam. Bake at 350 for 40-45 minutes. (I only bake mine for 25 minutes because my oven cooks hotter than most.)

FUDGE CUPCAKES

In memory of BERNADINE and MIKE TARVER. He grew the most beautiful roses and she was a marvelous cook and they shared!

1¾ **cups sugar** 1 **cup all-purpose flour** 4 **eggs** 4 **squares semi-sweet chocolate** 2 **sticks butter** 1½ **cups chopped pecans** 1 **teaspoon vanilla**	Combine sugar, flour and eggs. Blend by hand. Melt chocolate and butter in a saucepan. Add nuts. Add chocolate mixture to sugar mixture. Blend in vanilla. Do not beat. Pour batter into paper lined cupcake cups. Bake at 325 degrees 30 minutes.

CARAMEL PECAN ICING

Perfect for that fresh apple cake or an aromatic spice cake. I love the Duncan Hines spice cake mix, adding a little sprinkle or two of cinnamon, ground nutmeg and cloves.

1	**cup packed brown sugar**
4	**tablespoons butter**
¾	**cup evaporated milk**
2	**tablespoons butter**
1½	**cups chopped pecans**
1½	**cups powdered sugar**

Combine brown sugar, butter and milk in a saucepan. Bring to boil. Cook 2 minutes. Cool slightly. Melt butter in a small skillet. Add pecans and lightly toast. Add pecans and powdered sugar to brown sugar mixture. Mix well and cool slightly. Frost a cooled cake.

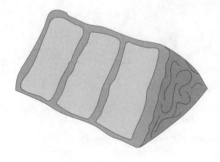

LEMON TEA CAKES

I had the privilege of hosting the Garden Party for the Methodist Children's Home in Ruston and serving on the next year's Under The Oaks party committee. We met at Goldmine Plantation, the home of BETTY and JAY CUMMINS. Betty sets the standard for hosting committee meetings! You immediately feel right at home when greeted with Betty's warm smile and the most wonderful scents imaginable-fresh hot coffee, a just out of the oven pound cake and freshly cut roses. At one of our meetings, she served these Lemon Tea Cakes with a lime sherbet float in darling old fashioned soda glasses along with sparkling sterling silver ice tea spoons and freshly ironed linen napkins. Queen Elizabeth could not to it any better!

2   **sticks unsalted butter, softened**
1   **cup sugar**
2   **egg yolks**
1   **teaspoon lemon zest**
2   **teaspoons lemon juice**
1   **teaspoon vanilla**
2   **cups all-purpose flour**

Cream butter and sugar. Stir in egg yolks. Add zest, juice, vanilla and flour. Mix well. Refrigerate. Roll out dough and cut into desired shapes. Bake at 325 degrees 15 to 20 minutes.

PECAN DAINTIES

*These are HELEN CORBITT'S and one of the most pop-
ular cookies on the tidbit tray during Tea Time at the
Zodiac restaurant at Neiman Marcus. When in Dallas,
I love lunch at the Zodiac. When seated, they bring you
a demitasse cup of the best hot chicken broth. A well
needed nourishment after a morning of shopping!*

*For all you young things who never heard of Helen
Corbitt, she was the Julia Child of Texas back in the
50's and 60's. She was a dear friend of my friends, the
TONY BRIGGLES. I was fortunate enough to dine with
her and entertained her several times. Her cookbook is
still one of my favorites.*

1   **egg white**
1   **cup packed light
      brown sugar**
1½ **cups pecan halves**

Beat egg white until stiff.
Gradually add brown sugar,
beating constantly. Slowly
fold in pecans. Drop dough
by teaspoons onto a greased
baking sheet. Bake at 250
degrees 30 minutes. Imme-
diately remove from baking
sheet and cool.

CRISPY OAT COOKIE

A great cookie! This recipe belongs to LUCY KLEIN-SCHMIDT, who married DICK SEIDENSPINNER, whose mother married MR. CRUTHIRDS! How are those names for the Deep South?

2   sticks butter,
    softened
1   cup sugar
1   cup packed brown
    sugar
1   egg
1   cup vegetable oil
1   teaspoon vanilla
3½ cups all-purpose flour
1   teaspoon baking soda
½   teaspoon salt
1   cup dry uncooked
    rolled oats
1   cup corn flakes cereal
1   cup chopped pecans

Cream butter. Gradually add sugar and brown sugar, beating at medium speed. Add egg, oil and vanilla. Mix well. In a separate bowl, combine flour, baking soda and salt. Add to creamed mixture. Stir in oats, cereal and nuts. Shape dough into 1-inch balls. Place on an ungreased baking sheet. Flatten with a fork. Bake at 325 degrees 15 minutes. Cool slightly and remove from baking sheet. Cool completely.

CHOCOLATE PECAN COOKIES

1   18-ounce package
     chocolate cake mix
1   3-ounce box instant
     vanilla pudding mix
1   egg, beaten
1   cup vegetable oil
1   cup finely chopped
     pecans
1   teaspoon vanilla

Combine cake mix, pudding mix, egg, oil, pecans and vanilla. Mix well. Do not refrigerate dough before baking because they will not hold together. Roll dough into marble size balls. Bake at 350 degrees 10 to 12 minutes. Cool slightly. Remove to racks.

It is best to wash and cool your baking sheet between batches to keep cookies from spreading too much. This recipe makes a lot of cookies so it is good to have large baking sheets.

Variation: To make Nut Butter Cookies, substitute yellow cake mix. Increase pecans to 1 1/4 cups and add 1 teaspoon butter flavoring instead of vanilla. Bake until lightly browned.

PECAN PETIT FOURS

Delicious served with scoops of vanilla ice cream or whipped cream.

Dough:

2 **cups all-purpose flour**	Combine flour, salt and
¼ **teaspoon salt**	sugar. Work in butter with
¼ **cup sugar**	hands or pastry blender.
2 **sticks butter, softened**	Add vinegar. Spread dough into a 15 x 10 x 1-inch bak-
2 **tablespoons white vinegar**	ing sheet, pushing up sides. Set aside.

Filling:

1½ **cups packed dark brown sugar**	Combine brown sugar, sugar, flour, salt, eggs, cream
½ **cup sugar**	and vanilla. Mix well. Add
2 **tablespoons all-purpose flour**	pecans. Pour filling over crust. Bake at 350 degrees
½ **teaspoon salt**	30 to 35 minutes or until
2 **eggs, beaten**	filling is set and caramel
¾ **cup heavy cream or evaporated milk**	colored. Cool completely. Cut into 2-inch squares.
½ **teaspoon vanilla**	
2½ **cups coarsely chopped pecans**	

LIZZIES

Emilie Jinks makes these best and a Huey holiday favorite! Great for that "just a bite of fruitcake".

8 ounces golden
   raisins, chopped
8 ounces currants
   or dark raisins,
   chopped
1 cup packed brown
   sugar
1 stick butter, softened
4 eggs, beaten
3 cups all-purpose flour
3 teaspoons baking
   soda
1 teaspoon ground
   allspice
1 teaspoon cinnamon
1 teaspoon ground
   nutmeg
3 tablespoons milk
1 cup bourbon
1 pound diced candied
   fruit, peel, chopped
8 ounces candied
   lemon peel,
   chopped
8 ounces candied
   cherries, chopped
4 cups chopped nuts

Soak raisins in hot water. Drain. Cream sugar and butter. Add eggs. Sift together flour, baking soda, allspice, cinnamon and nutmeg. Whisk together milk and bourbon. Add flour mixture alternately with bourbon mixture to creamed mixture. Add all fruit and nuts. Mixing well to coat. Drop batter by teaspoonfuls onto lightly greased baking sheets or fill mini muffin cups. Bake at 275 degrees 15 to 20 minutes.

ENGLISH ROCKS

Christmas time- MAMA made "rocks". I love my Mama!

¾ **cup firmly packed light brown sugar**
1 **stick butter, softened**
2 **large eggs**
1½ **cups all-purpose flour**
½ **teaspoon ground cinnamon**
½ **teaspoon baking soda**
¼ **teaspoon salt**
¼ **teaspoon ground cloves**
¼ **teaspoon ground allspice**
¼ **cup brandy**
2 **cups chopped pecans**
½ **pound candied cherries, halved**
½ **pound candied pineapple, chopped**
1 **cup pitted dates, chopped**
1 **cup raisins**

Beat brown sugar and butter at medium speed until smooth. Add eggs, beating until blended. In a separate bowl, combine flour, cinnamon, baking soda, salt, cloves and allspice. Gradually add to creamed mixture. Beat in brandy. Combine pecans, cherries, pineapple, dates and raisins in a large bowl. Pour batter over pecan mixture. Stir well. Drop batter by rounded teaspoonfuls, 2-inches apart, onto a lightly greased baking sheets. Bake at 325 degrees 20 minutes or until lightly browned. Cool 2 to 3 minutes. Remove from sheet to wire rack. Cool completely.

MRS. BOND'S ALMOND MACAROONS

BOND'S BAKERY, across the street from H. Mickel Dry Goods on Harrison Street, was an institution in Monroe for years.

1	**7-ounce roll almond paste**
¾	**cup sugar**
2	**small egg whites, slightly beaten**
1	**tablespoon all-purpose flour**
¼	**teaspoon almond extract, optional**

Beat paste and sugar. Add egg whites. Beat until smooth but not runny. Add flour and extract. Grease and flour a foil lined baking sheet. Spoon batter into a cake decorator bag with a star tip. Pipe batter into 1-inch diameter rounds. If you do not have a bag, spoon onto foil using a teaspoon. Leave enough room between for macaroons to double in size. Bake at 325 degrees 15 minutes or until golden brown. Cool on foil.

COCONUT MACAROONS

Mike and I ate our way through the tiny villages of France in the Alsace Loraine region. Each village had their own version of macaroons, all were so good and all a little different.

2	**egg whites**
2	**tablespoons cake flour**
½	**cup sugar**
¼	**teaspoon salt**
½	**teaspoon vanilla**
2	**cups shredded coconut**

Beat egg whites until stiff but not dry. Fold in flour, sugar and salt. Add vanilla and fold in coconut. Drop batter by teaspoonfuls onto a lightly greased parchment paper lined baking sheet. Bake at 350 degrees 20 minutes.

SWEET POTATO COOKIES

1½ sticks butter,
    softened
1   cup sweet potato,
    cooked and mashed
¾ cup packed brown
    sugar
½ cup sugar
1   egg
1½ cups all-purpose flour
1   teaspoon baking
    powder
¼ teaspoon cinnamon
½ teaspoon ground
    nutmeg
¾ cup quick cooking
    oatmeal
1   cup pecans
1   cup raisins

Cream butter, potato, brown sugar and sugar. Add egg and mix well. Add flour, baking powder, cinnamon, nutmeg, oatmeal, pecans and raisins. Drop batter by teaspoonfuls on a baking sheet. Bake at 350 degrees 10 to 12 minutes.

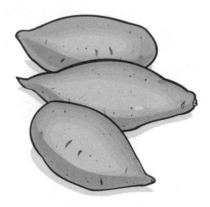

APPLE DUMPLINGS

My daughter-in-law, JANELLE SNELLINGS, fixed these for Thanksgiving. They were the hit and the best of the dessert table, which included homemade coconut cake, pecan pie, pumpkin pie, all outstanding desserts. This took first prize. These are so easy and something fun that children enjoy helping make.

2	apples, cut into 16 slices
2	8-ounce can refrigerated crescent rolls
2	sticks butter
2	cups sugar
1	12-ounce can lemon-lime carbonated beverage
	Cinnamon to taste

Separate rolls into 16 triangles. Roll up 1 apple slice in each triangle. Place in 13 x 9 x 2-inch baking dish. Melt butter in microwave. Add sugar and heat about 1 minute or until sugar dissolves. Pour butter mixture over dumplings. Pour beverage over all. Sprinkle with cinnamon. Bake at 350 degrees about 45 minutes or until dumplings are browned and syrup is thickened. Serve warm with a dollop of whipped topping or scoop of vanilla ice cream.

May also use peaches.

PEACH COBBLER

A MOLLY BROWN Special!

**3-4 cups sliced fresh
    peaches**
1   cup sugar
**½   teaspoon almond
    extract**
4   tablespoons butter
1   cup sugar
1   cup all-purpose flour
**½   tablespoon baking
    powder**
**   Pinch of salt**
¾   cup milk

Combine peaches, sugar and extract. Set aside. Melt butter in a 9-inch square baking dish in the oven. Combine sugar, flour, baking powder, salt and milk in a bowl. Blend until smooth. Pour batter over butter. Do not stir. Top with peach mixture. Do not stir. Bake at 350 degrees 1 hour or until golden brown. Batter will rise to top while baking.

Variation: Try combining ½ cup packed brown sugar and ½ cup sugar with peaches.

Variation: For Apple Cobbler, use two 16-ounce cans sliced apples mixed with 1 cup packed brown sugar, ⅓ cup apple juice and ½ teaspoon almond extract. Follow recipe as above.

SUPREME STRAWBERRY OR PEACH PIE

1	14-ounce can sweetened condensed milk
	Juice of 2 lemons or ½ cup
2	egg yolks
1	teaspoon vanilla
2	egg whites, beaten stiff
1	pint strawberries or peaches, sliced
1	10-inch pie crust, baked
1	cup heavy cream, whipped

Combine condensed milk and juice. Stir in egg yolks and vanilla. Fold in beaten egg whites and berries. Pour filling into crust. Bake at 275 degrees 10 to 15 minutes. Refrigerate. Top with whipped cream.

BLUEBERRY PIE

1	cup sour cream
2	tablespoons all-purpose flour
¾	cup sugar
1	teaspoon salt
1	large egg, beaten
2½	cups blueberries, rinsed and drained
	Pastry for 9-inch pie, unbaked
3	tablespoons all-purpose flour
3	tablespoons unsalted butter, softened
½	cup chopped pecans

Blend sour cream, flour, sugar, salt and egg. Fold in berries. Pour filling into pastry shell. Bake at 400 degrees 25 minutes. Combine flour, butter and pecans. Sprinkle mixture on top. Bake an additional 10 minutes. Refrigerate.

LEMON PIE IN THE SKY

EVAPORATED MILK...the milk that whips! Freeze the evaporated milk until crystals appear. It whips like whipping cream. Think of all those fat grams you are saving!

Years ago this recipe was given to me as a wedding present, with the pie in the glass dish that I still have. As a young bride, I loved to serve this. It was so wonderful and easy. As the years went by, life in general, (the good, the bad and the ugly), a divorce, several moves, the Gulf War and a big fire, I lost the recipe. The other day I was making banana pudding for MIKE CAGE, his favorite, and the recipe came to me. This is it, I am so excited! You can make this several days ahead. Remember, when entertaining, do as much ahead as possible. You want to enjoy your guests.

1½ **cups graham cracker or vanilla wafer crumbs**
2 **tablespoons sugar**
2-3 **tablespoons butter, melted**
1 **12-ounce can evaporated milk**
Juice of 2 big lemons
Zest of 2 lemons
1 **teaspoon almond extract**
1 **14-ounce sweetened condensed milk, may use fat free**
Zest of 1 lime
Garnish: mint or pretty pansies

Combine crumbs, sugar and butter, reserving ½ cup crumbs. Press mixture into a lightly greased pie plate or springform pan or ramekins. Pour evaporated milk into a small bowl. Freeze 30 minutes or until crystals form around the edges. Beat on high 1 to 2 minutes until very frothy. Gradually add juice, zest and extract. Beat 2 minutes until fairly stiff. Slowly beat in condensed milk. Beat 1 to 2 minutes. Pour filling over crust. Sprinkle with reserved crumbs, lemon and lime zest. Freeze. Remove

(Lemon Pie in the Sky, continued)

from freezer 10 minutes before serving. Garnish with mint or pansies.

Remember fat free products are loaded with sugar and lots of calories. In the long run calories are all that count. You must burn more calories than you take in or you are going to be fat. You know you do not like being a fatty and it is not healthy! It is hard on your heart, joints and look at all the people having knees and hips replaced from carrying around all that weight.

COCONUT MERINGUE PIE

2 cups milk
1 cup sugar
4 Tablespoons butter
½ cup all-purpose flour
4 eggs, separated
1 cup coconut flakes
   and more for top
1 teaspoon vanilla
1 9-inch pie crust,
   baked
4 egg whites
¼ teaspoon salt
¼ teaspoon cream of
   tartar or vinegar
⅔ cup sugar
   Garnish: Coconut
   flakes

Combine milk, sugar, butter, flour and egg yolks in a saucepan. Cook and stir over medium heat. When mixture starts to thicken, add coconut. Cook until thick. Remove from heat. Add vanilla. Beat until smooth. Pour filling into baked crust. In a bowl, beat egg whites until foamy. Add salt and cream of tartar. Continue beating and gradually add sugar until stiff peaks form. Spread meringue over filling, sealing edges. Sprinkle with coconut. Bake at 350 degrees until golden brown.

CHOCOLATE COVERED CHERRIES

Do not miss this, even if you think you do not like mara-schino cherries. JEAN MINTZ served these on a great big chocolate cake. It was so pretty and so unbeliev-ably good that I thought I was in Belgium!

3   10-ounce jars maraschino cherries, with stems, drained
1½ sticks butter
1   14-ounce can sweetened condensed milk
2   16-ounce packages powdered sugar
1   teaspoon salt
1   3½-ounce can coconut
2   cups pecans, finely chopped
4   cups semi-sweet chocolate chips
1   tablespoon vegetable oil

Drain cherries, pat dry and refrigerate 1 hour. Melt butter in a saucepan. Remove from heat and cool slightly. Pour butter into a large bowl. Add milk, sugar, salt, coconut and pecans. Mix well. This will be very stiff. Shape mixture into marble size balls. Flatten and wrap around cherries. Place covered cherry on wax paper. Cover loosely and refrigerate 1 hour. Melt chocolate with oil in a heavy saucepan. Stir until smooth. Hold each cherry by its stem and dip in warm chocolate. Set on wax paper to cool. May have to reheat chocolate. Pack cherries in layers separated by wax paper. Store in an airtight container in a cool place.

MEXICAN FUDGE OR MEXICAN ORANGE CANDY

My sweet friend CAROL RISPOLI shared this with me. This candy is like praline with a different twist. Everyone has a fit over them. I had these for a Christmas party and I think I saw PAT JORDAN put some in her purse and KEN FARRAR was helping her. Just kidding, they did say it was the very best they have had. There was none left!

4   **cups pecans**
4   **tablespoons butter, melted**
1   **tablespoon salt**
3½ **cups sugar**
1   **cup whole milk**
½   **cup sugar**
2   **tablespoons orange zest**
1   **tablespoon orange juice**

Combine pecans, butter and salt. Toast in the oven until lightly browned. Mix 3 1/2 cups sugar and milk in a saucepan. Bring to boil. Meanwhile, caramelize 1/2 cup sugar in a small iron skillet. Add to boiling mixture. Cook down to soft boil stage. Add pecans, zest and juice. Bring back to soft boil stage. Remove from heat and beat until mixture thickens. To test, see if mixture sits up and is not sticky. Spoon small scoops onto wax paper with thick newspaper underneath. Let cool. Pralines will lift right off. Store in airtight container for one week.

(Mexican Fudge or Mexican Orange Candy, continued)

To caramelize sugar, you need a small cast iron skillet. Heat to medium heat and add sugar. Do not leave the skillet for anything. When sugar begins to melt, stir until it turns that pretty caramel brown. Once it starts melting, it happens fast. This is very hot, be careful, have your hot pads handy.

To caramelize pecans, walnuts or almonds, add 1/4 cup water to this very hot mixture. Add nuts and mix well to coat. Pour into a colander, drain well and spread on a baking sheet. Separate nuts. These are really good in salads or as a snack.

HEAVENLY HASH

4   **cups sugar**
1   **cup cocoa powder**
1   **cup heavy cream**
½   **cup light corn syrup**
1   **stick butter**
½   **teaspoon salt**
2   **cups pecans, lightly toasted and chopped**
     Miniature marshmallows

Combine sugar, cocoa, cream and corn syrup in a saucepan. Bring to boil. Reduce heat and cool to soft boil stage or a candy thermometer reaches 240 degrees. Remove from heat. Add butter and salt. Beat until nearly cool and looks sugary and the color is dull. Add nuts. Pour half the mixture into a buttered 13 x 9 x 2-inch baking dish. Cover with marshmallows. Spread remaining mixture on top. Cool. Cut into squares.

Serve this on a pretty crystal plate garnished with small green holly sprigs for Christmas or springtime pansies.

DATE NUT LOAF

MAMA made this every Christmas. Childhood memories.

3 **cups sugar**
2 **tablespoons butter**
1 **cup milk**
1½ **pounds dates,**
   chopped
1½ **cups chopped nuts**
1 **teaspoon vanilla**

Combine sugar, butter, milk and dates in a saucepan. Cook and stir constantly. When mixture reaches 240 degrees on a candy thermometer or forms soft ball stage, remove from heat. Beat until thick. Add nuts and vanilla. Mix well. Pour mixture onto a damp cloth. Shape into a two loaves about 1½-inches in diameter and 8-inches long. Refrigerate. Slice when cold, as needed.

To check when candy has formed a soft ball, drop a bit of mixture in a cup of cold water. If it is right, it will make a little ball. Isn't that fun?

TOFFEE CHOCOLATE SQUARES

Easy! Tastes very much like a Heath bar.

Graham crackers
1   cup packed brown
       sugar
1   stick plus 2
       tablespoons butter
1   12-ounce package
       milk chocolate
       chips
1   cup ground pecans

Grease a 15 x 10 x 1-inch rimmed baking sheet. Line the bottom with separated rectangular crackers placed side by side. Combine brown sugar and butter in a saucepan. Simmer 3 minutes. Pour mixture quickly over crackers. Bake at 400 degrees 5 minutes. Remove from oven. Immediately, sprinkle with chocolate chips, spreading to cover as they melt. Top with pecans. Cool and cut into squares.

PEANUT BUTTER FUDGE

BETTY MADDRY shared this recipe with me and it is just wonderful!

2 cups sugar
1 cup evaporated milk
Dash salt
2 Tablespoons, white Karo syrup
½ stick of butter
4 Tablespoons peanut butter, smooth or crunchy

Boil to a soft roll. Turn off heat. Add butter and about four heaping tablespoons of peanut butter. Beat until creamy.

Pour into a buttered dish, allowing to cool. Cut it into squares and serve.

Drinks & Spirits

FOR THE LOVE OF TEA

Americans did not drink iced tea until 1904. During a heat wave at the St. Louis World's Fair, the hot tea vender at the Far East Pavilion was not doing much business. Some enterprising fellow tried pouring tea over ice and it was a hit. Down South, we like our tea with real sugar, fresh lemon and a sprig of fresh garden mint. I use Sweet and Low most of the time, but there is really no substitute for sugar.

Recently, green tea has become very popular because of the powerful antioxidants it contains. These antioxidants have been shown in recent studies to fight viruses, slow aging and have a beneficial effect on health.

Special Benefits of Green Tea:
Reduces high blood pressure
Lowers blood sugar
Fight cancer
Boosts the immune system
Lowers cholesterol

Who knows? If all this is true, it surely does sound like it is good for you!

To make the best tea, use your teapot. A teapot is best because it helps keep the water hot during brewing. If you do not have a teapot, use a container that you can cover while the tea is brewing.

Bring fresh cold tap water to full rolling boil. Water that has been reheated in a kettle gives tea a flat taste. Only boiling water poured over the tea produces the full flavor. Use one teaspoon of tea or one teabag per cup. Do not guess. A teabag is the equivalent of a teaspoon of loose tea.

Brew by the clock, 3 to 5 minutes, depending upon the strength you like. It takes time for the leaves to unfold and release their flavor, so do not guess.

(For the Love of Tea, continued)

Tea leaves and teabags are easy to keep fresh. Just be sure to put it in a tightly sealed canister or jar away from cooking odors and spices. It is best to keep tea no more than six months, as it will gradually lose its fine flavor. Tea used immediately after it is made, poured hot, has a lovely sparkling color. When made ahead, iced tea should be stored at room temperature. Storing tea in the refrigerator will cause it to cloud, but this is in no way harmful. It merely destroys the aesthetic qualities of clear tea.

A PASSION FOR COFFEE

As Irving Berlin sang "Let's have another cup of coffee. Coffee in the morning and kisses in the night." Sounds like a good idea to me!

A good cup of coffee is a must. Buy the proper grind for the coffee maker. Dark and light roast is a matter of taste but make sure to buy a high-quality bean. I like Community or Starbucks. Use 2 rounded tablespoons coffee (more for a stronger brew) to 12 ounces of good water. Store your coffee in an airtight container. Coffee exposed to air loses it aroma. You will never fool anyone with warmed-over coffee, so do not try. At least once a week rub the inside of your pot with baking soda, then run vinegar through your coffee maker followed by cold water. In other words, make sure you have a clean, fresh coffee pot!

Put hot water in your coffee mugs or cups to warm them. When ready to serve, pour out the hot water and pour in your coffee. This is especially nice to do on chilly mornings!

ICE RING OF FLOWERS OR FRUIT

Let's be fancy!

A flower or fruit ice mold with pretty baby ivy is hard to beat in your bowl. These are fun and easy to make. Remember, boiled water makes a clearer mold.

First select a mold in keeping with the size of your punch bowl so there will be room for dipping punch. Put 3 to 4 inches of water in your mold and freeze. Select your fruits or flowers. I love to use bunches of red and green grapes with pretty mint and petit-point ivy. Add a little more water and freeze. Repeat until full and freeze. When you are ready to remove the ring, hold it in a pan of hot water for just a minute. You can also pour water 2/3 of the way into ice trays and freeze. Remove ice cubes and pour in drinks or punch bowl. Looks so pretty!

Once for DEANIE BAKER'S Birthday lunch, I took a fifth of Bombay Gin, placed it in a half gallon milk carton, added water, baby ivy and grapes. When it was frozen, I just peeled the container away. Place the mixture in a shallow bowl with more ivy and add some flowers. I used it as the centerpiece and Deanie's birthday present. It was pretty and fun and she was tickled.

DAZZLE YOUR GUESTS WITH CHAMPAGNE!

When Mike and I toured France several years ago, we went to Reims and visited several of the vineyards where some of the best wines in the world are made. The scenery is just breathtaking and the people are all very friendly. Maybe this is why Reims is the home of everyone's favorite celebration spirit – champagne!

The locals in the region are very quick to point out that all sparkling wines are not champagne, even though some call themselves that. Legally, a sparkling wine (wine with bubbles) can only be called champagne if it is made in the Reims Region of France. So even though vineyards in California produce some very nice "sparkling wines," it's not champagne unless it comes from Reims.

I also picked up a few tips about serving champagne. Always chill glasses before serving. Use only small amounts of liqueur or mixers, so you don't overwhelm the flavor of the sparkling wine or champagne. Pour your mixer into the glass first and then add the wine. Use quality but not expensive champagnes or sparkling wines, preferably in the range of $8-15 per bottle. Always serve champagne chilled. Small strips of citrus peel and other garnishes that don't get in the way of sipping make a wonderful finishing touch! Here are a few recipes to get your own champagne celebration kicked off!

Classic Champagne Cocktail:
Champagne
Sugar cube
Angostura bitters
Lemon peel
Orange wedge

Place sugar cube in champagne flute and saturate with bitters. Pour in champagne, twist lemon peel over drink and drop it into glass along with orange wedge.

Kir Royale:
Champagne
teaspoon cassis, frambois liqueur, or Chambord
Champagne

Pour liqueur into champagne glass and fill with champagne.

Bellini:
Puréed White Peach
Dashes of lemon juice
Dashes of peach brandy
Champagne

Stir peach, lemon juice and brandy in champagne flute. Fill glass with champagne.

MINT SYRUP

Delicious to make and keep in your refrigerator during those long hot summer months.

2   cups sugar
2½ cups water
    Juice of 6 lemons
    Zest of 2 oranges
    Juice of 2 oranges
4   large handfuls mint,
    rinsed

Dissolve sugar in water. Bring to boil for 10 minutes. Pour hot syrup over juices and mint. Cover and let steep several hours. Strain. Pour into jars and refrigerate.

May store refrigerated for several weeks. Use in iced tea, mixed drinks or freeze to a slush and serve in sherbet glasses. Perfect for your mint juleps.

MARGARITAS

No one makes these better than Bob Cudd of Taos!

1   **part Gold Tequila**
    Equal parts fresh
      lime juice and bar
      syrup or Margarita
      mix
½   **part Cointreau or**
      triple sec
    Ice and salt
	Combine Tequila, juice, bar syrup, Cointreau and ice. Shake well. Wet rim of glass and invert on a heavily salt-ed towel. Pour mixture into glasses and serve.

MAGNOLIAS

Perfect for your Bridesmaid's luncheon.

4   **cups fresh squeezed**
      sweet orange juice,
      chilled
1   **bottle Champagne,**
      chilled, not
      expensive
½   **cup Grand Marnier or**
      Orange
    Curacao
    Garnish: Orange curls
      and mint
	Just before serving, mix juice and Champagne. Pour into individual glasses. Drizzle with a little Grand Marnier. Garnish with curls and mint.
	
	Tie a pretty ribbon around the base of your Champagne flutes for a nice touch.

TEQUILA SUNRISE

The name comes from the multi-colored layers, resembling a sunrise! Wonderful and pretty!

1½ **ounces tequila**
½ **cup orange juice**
2 **teaspoons lime juice**
1 **ounce Grenadine**
   Garnish: Orange slice
   and Maraschino
   cherry

Combine tequila, orange juice and lime juice in a cocktail shaker with ice cubes. Shake until well chilled. Strain into a tall slender glass. Pour Grenadine down the side of the glass. Do not stir. Garnish with orange slice and cherry.

PINK SQUIRREL

A MUST for wild game dinners! October is a good time to clean out your game freezer. I do not like to keep game over a year. If you have not used it by now, you probably will not. It is going to have freezer burn. Shame on you. Give it away while it is still good. It is a sin to waste. Cook it up for a church supper or something like that. You could call it a Critter Cooking!

½ **ounce white crème de**
   cacao
½ **ounce half-and-half**
½ **ounce crème de**
   noyaux
   Crushed ice

Combine crème de cacao, half-and-half, crème de noyaux and ice in a shaker. Shake well. Strain into 3-ounce cocktail glass.

RASPBERRY SMASH

½   cup raspberries
3   tablespoons
    Chambord, black
    raspberry liqueur
2   teaspoons sugar
1   Champagne or
    sparkling wine,
    chilled

Gently mix raspberries, Chambord and sugar in a bowl. To soften, cover and refrigerate at least 1 hour and up to 2 hours. Spoon 2 tablespoons raspberries and juice into two Champagne flutes. Slowly top off with Champagne.

WASSAIL PUNCH

Smells like the holidays and puts you in a festive mood!

1   gallon apple cider
1   quart orange juice
1   cup lemon juice
1   quart pineapple juice
24 whole cloves
4   sticks cinnamon
1   cup sugar

Combine cider, all juices, cloves, cinnamon sticks and sugar in a large saucepan. Simmer 10 to 20 minutes. Remove cloves and cinnamon sticks. Serve warm in punch cups.

For a festive punch bowl, float small oranges that have been precooked about 10 minutes. Stick several cloves in each orange.

WHITE SANGRÍA

1⅓ cups water
½ cup sugar
4 3-inch cinnamon sticks
1 cup mint leaves, divided
1 750-ml bottle dry white wine
2 lemons, sliced
2 oranges, sliced
2 peaches, peeled and sliced
2 cups club soda, chilled

Combine water, sugar, cinnamon and ½ cup mint leaves in a saucepan. Bring to boil. Reduce heat and simmer 5 minutes. Remove from heat and cool. Cover and let stand 8 hours. Remove cinnamon sticks and mint leaves with a slotted spoon. Combine sugar mixture, remaining mint leaves, wine, lemon slices, orange slices and peach slices in a large pitcher. Refrigerate overnight. Just prior to serving, add club soda. Serve over ice.

FIVE-FRUIT CRUSH

¾ cup sliced ripe bananas
½ cup chopped, peeled ripe mango
2 cups whole strawberries
¾ cup pineapple juice, chilled
½ cup orange juice, chilled
½ cup ice cubes

Place banana and mango slices in the freezer about 1 hour. Remove from freezer. Let stand 10 minutes. Combine strawberries and juices in a blender. Process until smooth. With blender running, add one piece at a time of bananas, mangos and ice cubes. Process until smooth. Serve immediately.

Lagniappe

Gardening and Living

LYoung

JANUARY

I love the stark beauty of winter. Those messy sycamore trees are so beautiful this time of year, with their white-barked limbs. Dogwood trees take on a special winter beauty, all bare and showing off those red seed pods. And the winter brings millions of migrating blackbirds to this area. I'm glad we live in an area with seasonal change!

Let's work on getting into good shape! During the holidays, you can gain 8 to 15 pounds. Most people burn 1800 to 2200 calories a day. With the holidays, its easy to eat 10,000 calories a day. That is over two pounds! Remember, 3500 calories equals one pound.We have to watch what we eat and count calories. Everything in MODERATION. Don't deprive yourself, just watch it. Read those labels, eat half of what you are served and write down every bite that goes in your mouth. When we are on a good program, don't we feel so much better? Losing 5 or 10 pounds, OH YES! We have to feel good so we can relish the moment and celebrate LIFE!

Remember these words, as you are going to hear them a lot! MODERATION, EXERCISE, and DRINK lots of GOOD WATER!

Menus for January

Cabbage Soup (pg.56)
Try this soup for 4 or 5 days and
just watch the pounds fall off!

Oyster Stew (pg. 60)

Gardening for January

1.) Bring into your home blooming Paper Whites or amaryllis.

2.) This is the month for moving or planting shrubs, trees, and vines.

3.) Plant your refrigerated Tulips.

4.) Get your MARTIN HOUSES cleaned out, the SCOUTS are coming!

5.) Don't forget to feed the birds.

6.) Scout the woods for SIMLAX. With all of those bare trees, it's easy to spot! Simlax is at its best in the fall and winter and perfect for the holiday parties and decorations. Using smilax in early spring is tricky, as the new growth is very fragile and will not hold up.

FEBRUARY
Roses are Red, Violets are blue,
Sugar is Sweet, and so are you!

Happy Valentine's Day and Fun Mardi Gras! I can never decide if I want to decorate for Valentines or Mardi Gras. We have lots of fun things to look forward to in February.

"Bless a thing and it will bless you. Curse it and it will curse you. If you bless a situation, it has no power to hurt you and if it is troublesome for a time, it will fade out, if you sincerely bless it." – Emmet Fox

In February, it is cold and wet; then we have beautiful sunshiny days. Down here in the Deep South, we can have a big wood burning fire one day and spring house cleaning the next. One thing is for sure: our weather is never boring!

I love this saying: NOTHING TASTES AS GOOD AS THIN FEELS!

Mike and I have really gotten serious about this SUGAR BUSTERS, SOUTHBEACH, and ATKINS idea. The more you read the more it makes sense! You really can have just about all of your favorites. Well, maybe not all. Chicken n' dumplings, cornbread, and pretty much anything white (potatoes and rice and sugar) are off the menu. But there are lots of really wonderful substitutes. Whole wheat pasta and brown rice are excellent choices and very satisfying. You need to read everything you can and try to put it all together for what works best for you.

Menus for February

Oyster & Artichoke Soup
(Cooking & Gardening, pg. 51)

Toasted Broccoli Salad (pg. 41)

Spinach Soufflé
(Cooking & Gardening, pg. 163)

Leg of Lamb
(Cooking & Gardening, pg. 212)

Rice, hot and fluffy, with the lamb gravy

Hot, Crusty French Bread

Fallen Chocolate Cake (pg. 150)

Gardening for February

1. Feed and enjoy the birds. Look for the Martin scouts. Watch for the Wood Ducks looking for a home.

2. Now is the season to work on your landscape design. Look around and steal ideas from books, magazines, and neighbors.

3. Time to trim liriope and mondo grass. Be careful not to cut it too low, because you may damage new growth.

4. Treat yourself to a pair of Weedeater 6-volt Shrub Clipper Grass Sheers. I just love the cordless electric power!

5. It is time to set out onion sets, cauliflower, cabbage, and broccoli. Fertilize all of your shrubs and trees and lawns too!

MARCH

March is dedicated to my old friend Linda Brice Sheppard, who passed away March 11. I am going to share this story with you because something very special happened, twelve days before her death. I had not heard from Linda in many years, my phone rang, it was Linda, said her favorite thing in Delta Style was my column, she always enjoyed it. She began by telling me things that were a part of my life and I had forgotten all about. Did the memories come back! I grew up playing on the Ouachita River, it was my backyard. We had a wonderful house boat with a big deck on the front and a Johnson 25 tied on the back and Daddy let us drive (have you heard that song) and we skied up and down that river without a sign of a ski belt, they didn't have them back then or either we did not have any. There was always a cooler full of ice cold drinks and a bar-b-q pit that never stopped smoking. When the weekend rolled around the Kings were heading to the River, There were four of us children, I have an older brother and two little sisters and mama let each invite a friend to go up the river, let me tell you, it was a coveted invitation with the Georgia Tucker and Neville friends. Having an older brother that I tagged along with, I guess you could call me a tomboy. We floated the river in the spring when it was high and fast, walked the bridges, loved to climb under the Louisiville Bridge and jump in and float to Howard Griffins boat dock. O what fun we had! Linda and I were in the 4th grade at Georgia Tucker. One Saturday we went to the movie at the old Delta Theater. Whoever was suppose to pick us up that afternoon did not show up and we had spent our last nickel. Every Saturday my Grandmother, Ruby Baker who lived in West Monroe, got Willie, her yard man, to get ole Bessie, her 1950 Chevy out of the garage, wash and shine her up. This was the day she dressed up, girdle and all and. ran her errands. In the .afternoon she would stop by the Trenton Street Bar for a visit and a cool one. Linda and I walked across the railroad bridge to find Mother Baker and a ride home. She had just left for Elsie Webb's. Jack the bar tender gave us a coke and sent us on our way. We crossed the Louisiville Bridge and on to my grandmother Breards on K and North 3 rd street. She was not home, but

she did have a charge account at Culpeppers Grocery, which was right behind her house. We got us a candy bar and ice cream and walked on to Linda's house on Forsythe. Needless to say her parents were hysterical. When Linda saw her Daddy's face, her face turned as red as the red jeans she was wearing. I did not see Linda much after that afternoon as she was forbidden to play with me but when I did see her, we would get tickled! O what sweet innocent times those were! This February 28th that Linda called, thinking back, she called to say goodbye. Linda had cancer, she did not tell me, she sounded wonderful, we just laughed and talked about old times. She said the bravest thing she ever did was her Saturday with me.... I asked her about someone very special to her (she had called me, maybe 20 years ago to do a favor for this person, or I would have not known about him) said she had not talked to him in several years, I said, you know time is a great healer and things will work out... I talked to this person and she called him the same day she called me and they did make up and had two wonderful visits.. Linda was saying goodbye to the people she loved and I am thrilled she loved me.....

Menus for March

Potatoes...Ouachita River Style....

When we were children going up the river, on the LONG-JOHNSILVER sandbar, which was my favorite, Daddy would dig a big pit, fill it with charcoal, throw a grill over and cook the best sirloin you ever had. Mama would take big Irish potatoes wrapped in foil and tuck them in the red hot coals. WONDERFUL! But the best part was the next week, the left over potatoes that Mama kept in the icebox and would fry.

4 large Irish potatoes, wash, dry and wrapped in foil. Bake in a 400 degree oven until done and then refrigerate until ready to use. These will keep about a week. When ready to cook, heat fresh oil, Wesson or peanut oil in your big black iron skillet. Remove the potatoes from the foil and slice about

⅛ of an inch thick and fry until golden brown. Drain on lots of paper towel. Salt and serve hot and crispy. These were my children's favorites! Good with a grilled steak and a big ice cold green salad with a blue cheese dressing.

Shrimp Dip Ella Mae (pg. 10)

Ice Cold Iceberg Lettuce Wedge
with a Blue Cheese Dressing (pg. 34)

Gardening for March

1.) Plant Hydrangea in partial shade to mostly shade. Fertilize and mulch with oak leaves or pine straw. Lime will keep them pink and sulphur will keep them a pretty blue. Don't forget the Oak-Leaf Hydrangea. It is the first to bloom in the Spring and makes big, pretty white blooms!

2.) Continue to plant Gladiolus and you can still set out Dahlias.

3.) Fertilize your Sweet Peas! Also, now is a great time to set out patches of grass. Centipede or St. Augustine.

APRIL

"The Angel of the Months"

With Passover, Good Friday and Easter, there is a celebration for everyone!

A few years back, my friend JEAN MINTZ was preparing her fabulous family dinner for their Hanukkah celebrations. I asked what she was serving and every dish sounded wonderful. When we got around to desserts, I was thinking that a crème brule on floating island would have been perfect. But she smiled and said that her grandchildren had requested one of their favorites – Banana Pudding. What better dessert is there than a banana pudding? And it's a family favorite too! For our holiday celebration of these most important holidays, let's prepare family favorites.

Gardening for April

1.) Now is the time to be a WILDCHILD in the garden! April is HERE! My favorite things for April are in Cooking & Gardening with Dianne.

2.) Trim and prune the shrubs that have bloomed such as azaleas, forsythias, quince and spiraeas after they have finished blooming. If you wait until summer to cut them back, you will remove next year's blooms. Speaking of SPIRAEA and, as the old saying goes, there are a thousand ways to go. I think azaleas without spiraeas sprinkled in is like a cake without icing! The spiraeas are like waves of fine old Belgium Lace. I just love it. It is not pretty in the winter, though, so be sure to tuck it in among your azaleas and evergreens.

3.) Making scents in your garden: Don't forget to include CAROLINA JASMINE and CONFEDERATE JASMINE in your garden. Put sweet scented plants close to the entrance of your home. Summer Phlox is wonderful and fragrant as well. It comes back every year in a variety of colors such as lavender, pink, rose and white. Also, Four O'Clocks (some people call them P.M.s) are so pretty and sweet smelling. But they can take over your garden. They are like bad little children—you have to watch them.

4.) It is time to plant a small vegetable garden. We like tomatoes, peppers, okra and eggplant. Try the Jerusalem Artichokes. They are a member of the Sunflower family, also known as "sunchoke." It is a rooted perennial, better adapted to the northern parts of the United States more than the South. Various Indians grew it for centuries as a staple food. Do not confuse it with the globe artichoke but it has the same flavor. Russ and Gail Bulloch shared with us several years ago and I have fallen in LOVE with them. They are great in stews or anything you bake in sauce and gravy. I have seen several recipes for a Jerusalem Artichoke Relish that looks really good! You plant in the spring and harvest in the fall. The artichokes will keep 3 or 4 months in the

refrigerator. They are a perennial, but planting is dif-
ficult to maintain through warm winters. So down here
in the Deep South, you most probably will have to get a
new start.

Over half of the carbohydrates they contain is in the
form of inulin and this cannot be absorbed by the body.
It does mean you can eat quite a lot without putting on
weight, but it also means that many people will find the
inulin fermenting in their gut, which can cause quite a
bit of wind! The tubers can be eaten raw or cooked and
the flavor improves if they are left in the ground until
the frost. If you want to know more about this JERU-
SALEM ARTICHOKE, GOOGLE it! My how times have
changed with the world of the computer!

5.) This is a good time of year to plant TREES. Nothing is
more beautiful than a MAGNOLIA and there is nothing I
love more than bringing in the big, fragrant blossoms in
May and June. They just make your whole house smell
good and what in the world would we do without the
magnificent foliage for all our decorating? A magnolia
tree is very messy. NEVER cut the limbs up. You want
them flowing onto the ground. Or, as RENE CASCIO,
our 2005 president of the MONROE GARDEN CLUB
says, "a skirt all the way to the ground." Once you cut
the lower limbs, they will never grow back. Leaving the
limbs on the ground, the tree will litter within itself. No
one wants to mow around or under a Magnolia; the big
seed pods and the tough leaves are rough on a mower.
With that in mind and the size of the big tree, find the
right place in your landscape design, but you need a big
yard.

6.) Be patient, be patient! It is almost time to plant your
impatiens, caladiums, peppers, and tomatoes. You can
get your beds ready and I know your PANSIES are still
pretty, so enjoy! If you cannot wait, you could plant pe-
tunias, snapdragons, sweet Williams and nasturtiums
(one of my grandmother's very favorite)!

MAY

I do love May; it is truly one of the most beautiful months of the year! How many of you remember the MAYPOLE? It is a tall flowered wreath-pole forming a center for May Day sports and dances. It would be fun to do one for a special occasion.

You learn something everyday. I never knew it, but I'm a PRESERVATIONIST! A group of GEORGIA TUCKER alums are working really hard to save our magnificent old grammar school. It was built in 1918. I graduated from Georgia Tucker in 1955 and way in the back of my mind I remember we had a maypole celebration and it was so much fun.

CINCO DE MAYO a good reason to have a MEXICAN PARTY! Try and find a Mariachi Band. Usually they are in the area this time of the year for the Mexican Restaurants May celebration! If you cannot find a band, get some good Mexican fiesta music! Get your piñatas out and all Mexican decorations. Make a list of friends. A fun invitation is a must; it sets the pace for your party, now lets start cooking and planning. Gather small terracotta shot glasses with a little handle on each one. Tie a thin 24 inch colorful ribbon on the handle, long enough to slip over each guest's head. Have a table, covered with serapes, where your guests will be arriving. Splurge and get several fine sipping tequilas. As each guest arrives, place a shot glass around their neck and give them a good splash of tequila. We are getting off to a good start! Continue with Margaritas, Mexican beer with fresh limes, salsa with tostadas and Pico de Gallo, guacamole, tacos, Mexican salad, enchiladas and pralines for dessert.

TOMATOES, once you have harvested your tomatoes, avoid refrigerating them. Cold temperature destroys both the flavor and texture of the fruit. I know, I know. They all come at one time. Well, have them for every meal or as much as

you can stand of such a fabulous gift from the GODS. Mike and I have BLT'S, TOMATO PIE, or THICK SLICES with homemade mayonnaise or French dressing with thin slices of purple onion and avocado. There is just nothing better. YUM, YUM!!! You should get on BETTY EARLE and BOB ERLE CLARK'S tomato list! (Oak Ridge Connection!)

Gardening in May

Plant your caladiums. There isn't a beautiful garden in the South that doesn't have caladiums. Try and get all your bedding plants in and well established, hot and dry is on the way! Don't forget 100 sweet cherry tomatoes!

Plant a MAYPOP; it is a climbing perennial passionflower that just loves the Deep South. The blooms look like an exotic plant from maybe the moon.

JUNE

Let's seize the moment and celebrate JUNE! Take time to enjoy your beautiful yard! Be sure and get a big sweet WATERMELON and chill it for a couple of days. For a party once, we cut plugs around the melon, maybe 2 or 3 and poured a fifth of vodka in, replaced the plugs and chilled for a couple of days. Did our guest enjoy that watermelon? You bet! A good time was had by all.

The old timers say when the bitter pecans start to bud out in the river bottoms, you look for pecan worms. They are found only on the bitter pecan trees. As these worms fall off the trees into the river, WATCH OUT! That is where the bream are. We can catch all we want. Talk about fun! Now that we have fresh fish, let's cook!

What's for SUPPER? I have got the beefsteak, porksteak, the mutton and the lamb; stewed Irish potatoes, salty frog and ham. I have them on the griddle and they are piping hot with onion in the middle and a tomato on the top! PASS THE BUTTER! This sounds like Grand Paw Jones or maybe Wayne Taunton.

Menus for June

Southern Fried Fish
(Cooking & Gardening, pg. 229)

Try mealing your fish in "Cream Meal"!

Tartar Sauce
(Cooking & Gardening, pg. 95)

Fresh Purple Hull Peas

Fresh Thick Slices of Homegrown Tomatoes

Thin Slices of Cold Purple Onions

Gardening for June

Plant WHEAT GRASS in large or small containers for table decorations. My friend Linda Trinca grew a 5 by 10 foot table cloth of wheat for her daughters wedding announcement party. They covered the table with several layers of heavy plastic, laid the grass on top. The center piece was a big, interesting shape. A big log with mushrooms and fungi mixed in with a glass turtle that looked so real. The food was served on crystal platters and bowls. SPECTULAR! Linda said she started the grass cloth about 3 weeks before the party, she trimmed it several times. To place the cloth, they rolled it up and it took 4 men to help place it.

Plant lots of CREPE MYRTLES. They will bloom when nothing else will!

JULY

It's hot but the cotton is growing! The 4th of July is coming, so let's celebrate with lots of fireworks and a backyard barbeque.

Menus for July

Grilled Cabrito
Let's cook goat!

Potato Salad
(Cooking & Gardening, pg. 82)

Deviled Eggs (pg. 73)

Thick Slices of Fresh Garden Tomatoes!

Chocolate Sheet Cake
(Cooking & Gardening, pg. 275)

Ice Cold Watermellon

Gardening for July

1.) Water, Water, Water!

2.) Time to plant multiplying green onions.

3.) Cut back leggy annuals. They will come back full and pretty and you will be able to enjoy them until the first frost.

4.) Find a shady spot and read a good book.

5.) Throw avocado seeds in "flower beds".

AUGUST

Mother Nature teases us with hints of FALL!

If at all possible, travel someplace where it is cool. I'm worried about this GLOBAL WARMING! I guess what we can to do to help is be a good steward of our environment. It is just a NANO-drop in the bucket but as the old saying goes, "every little bit helps".

Lets have friends over for SUNDAY SUPPER. You can prepare most of this ahead of time. Make a list of fun friends.

I can seat 12 at my table comfortably but I like to have 3 to 4 couples but if it works out with 6, counting me and Mike that is fine too! Sometimes you have to call 10 couples to get 5, we are all so busy and in and out of town. It makes for a good party to have fun and special guest with common interest.

Set your table. Get Aunt Stella's big cut crystal bowl out and fill it with a small Magnolia branch, with the pretty green seed pod, mix in a few green and white caladium leaves and maybe a white or green hydrangea or two. WALLA! You have a beautiful, cool table arrangement. I know, I know. You are worried about chipping or breaking the wonderful old crystal bowl. If you do, so what? You have enjoyed and as the saying goes, "you didn't go to do it." I believe in using and enjoying my things. You'd better, because when you die your children most likely will put them in a garage sale!

Menus for August

Fall is on the way, DUCK SEASON around the corner; let's cook some those $200.00 Mallards in the freezer.

Stuffed Italian Artichokes
(Cooking & Gardening, pg. 173) For a appetizer

Wild Italian Duck Tetrazini (pg. 113)

The Best Green Salad
(Cooking & Gardening, pg. 79)
or
Caesar Salad
(Cooking & Gardening, pg. 78)

Garlic Bread

Venice Peaches
(Cooking & Gardening, pg. 247)

Gardening for August

1.) This is a good time to transplant Iris. Fertilize with bone meal.

2.) And it's still hot. So remember: Water, Water, Water!

SEPTEMBER

September, the harvest month...Summer is over and autumn has arrived.

> *Autumn to winter, winter to spring,*
> *Spring into summer, spring into fall-*
> *So rolls the changing year, and so we change;*
> *Motion so swift, we know not that we move*

~Author unknown

Up in the morning and off to school. Going to obey the GOLDEN RULE. "Do tee do...do tee do," as James Brown sings! We love to sing SONNY GOLDENROD, "Tell me, sonny goldenrod growing everywhere, did fairies come from fairyland and weave the golden dress you wear?"

Menus for September

Spanish Green Beans
(Cooking & Gardening, pg. 170)

Potato Casserole Wendy
(Cooking & Gardening, pg. 185)

Grilled Doves
(Cooking & Gardening, pg. 203)

Come on! You know how to grill doves. But if not, Mike Cage's 'Grilled Jalapeño Stuffed Duck Breast' works great for doves!

Chocolate Cookies
or

Neiman Marcus Brownies
(Cooking & Gardening, pg. 295)

Gardening for September

Dress your house for Fall! Buy Crotons in pots for partly-shaded patio or entrance areas. The brilliant reds, yellows, and greens are so pretty for Fall. I love to mix them with pumpkins, hay, sugar cane, gourds, and peppers.

The Red Spider Lilies are blooming! They always remind me of our sweet children going back to school. "They are like children. They are everywhere!" Be careful and watch out for them.

It's time to cut firewood. Confucius say, "man who cuts his own firewood, warms himself twice!" Mike Cage likes this one!

Fertilize your Chrysanthemums weekly until the flower buds show color. From then on, just water them. Also, fertilize your Wisteria and watch for fungus.

After a good rain, dig up your Caladiums. I use a big yard fork. Spread them out to dry. Store in airy baskets in a dry place...potting shed, storage room, etc., to protect from freeze. Always label color and variety. Believe me, you'll forget!

As annuals fade, take them up and prepare the beds for Fall.

Think about ordering your Paper Whites and Amaryllis for Christmas blooms.

OCTOBER

I love fall. FOOTBALL, tailgating, hunting season, the wonderful weather. Life is GOOD! So let's COOK.

The fields of harvest are bare,
And winter whistles through the square.
October dresses in flame and gold
Like an old woman afraid of growing old.

~Anne Lawler

October is MUFFIN and BISCUIT month. They keep well and are so easy to share with others!

Menus for October

Cocktail Weiners (pg. 30)

Curried Pumpkin Soup (pg. 54)

Sweet Potato Muffins or Pumpkin Bread
(Cooking & Gardening, pg. 135)

Cheese Puffs (pg. 31)

October is a good time to gather pine cones, cattails (to preserve, spray them with hairspray), and Tallow Berries (cut just as they begin to open) for your Fall and holiday decorations.

Gardening for October

1.) Cut back perennials like Banana plants and Elephant Ears. Divide and reset.

2.) Plant early blooming sweet peas and Forget-Me-Nots.

3.) Prune and take up Hibiscus plants before the frost gets them.

4.) Order tulips and refrigerate 4 to 6 weeks before planting.

5.) Plant Anemones ("eye up") and Ranunceulus ("feet down").

6.) Stir and water your compost pile.

NOVEMBER

November is here and I just love it. THE HOLIDAYS! Oh, yes! This time of the year I get so excited, the smell of a wood burning fire place, fall colors, the leaves falling. (I love raking them up, Mike Cage likes to mow them, said it is good mulch for the yard. He is fast on that lawn mower too!) We know all is right with the world. I think Walt Whitman said that. It is time to pick up PECANS, be sure and freeze plenty for the coming year. They will keep 2 or 3 years in the freezer, but I do like to use mine year to year. Hunting season is here, this is a good time to have friends and family over for dinner.

Lets clean that freezer out and be good STEWARDS of our game that we worked so hard to bag. How about a CRITTER cooking, a wild game dinner?

Menus for November

Fried Duck Breast with a Jezabel Sauce

Smoked Venison Roast

Grilled Doves (pg. 115)

Hot Cheese Grits (pg. 98)

Marinated Green Beans (pg. 93)

Hot Crusty French Bread

Pink Squirrel (pg. 183)

Hot Coffee

THANKSGIVING! We all have our old family favorites; turkey, dressing, rice and gravy, little green peas, cranberry salad, hot homemade rolls and of course pumpkin pie, with real whipped cream, pecan pie, and maybe a good fresh coconut cake! We have lots to be thankful for! Don't forget, TAKE EVERTHING IN MODERATION and a good long walk in the afternoon. ENJOY!

COCONUT CAKE (*Cooking & Gardening, pg. 279*)

PUMPKIN PIE (*Cooking & Gardening, pg. 306*)

GARDENING FOR NOVEMBER

PANSIES.... Now is the time... I just love them... plant now, with lots of bone meal and blood meal.. You will enjoy until late spring. You can be an **artist** with all the different colors and sizes. Pansies love cold weather, so you can even wait to plant them in late December or early January.

DECEMBER

Merry Christmas!

Desiderata

Go placidly amid the noise and haste and remember what peace there may be in silence. As far as possible without surrender be on good terms with all persons. Speak your truth quietly and clearly; and listen to others; even the dull and ignorant; they too have their story.

Avoid loud and aggressive persons, they are vexatious to the spirit. If you compare yourself with others, you may become vain and bitter; for always there will be greater and lesser persons than yourself. Enjoy your achievements as well as your plans.

Keep interested in your own career however humble; it is a real possession in the changing fortunes of time. Exercise caution in your business affairs; for the world is full of trickery. But let this not blind you to what virtue there is; many persons strive for high ideals; and everywhere life is full of heroism. Be yourself. Especially, do not feign affection. Neither be cynical about love; for in the face of all aridity and disenchantment it is perennial as the grass.

Take kindly the counsel of the years, gracefully surrendering the things of youth. Nurture strength of spirit to shield you in sudden misfortune. But do not distress yourself with imaginings. Many fears are born of fatigue and loneliness. Beyond a wholesome discipline, be gentle with yourself.

You are a child of the universe, no less than the trees and the stars; you have a right to be here. And whether or not it is clear to you, no doubt the universe is unfolding as it should.

Therefore be at peace with God, whatever you conceive Him to be, and whatever your labors and aspirations, in the noisy confusion of life keep peace with your soul. With all its sham, drudgery and broken dreams, it is still a beautiful world. Be cheerful. Strive to be happy. *~Max Ehrmann, 1927*

A HOLIDAY BUFFET!

Oysters Caribbean

Standing Rib Roast

Spinach

Curry Fruit

Cheese Grits

Homemade Rolls

Floating Island

Remembering Mama

Ella Mae Baker
King
1921

I grew up in Monroe on the Ouachita River. This section is just a collection of happy memories, fun stories and good tips! ENJOY!

I wanted to name this section "MY MAMA DONE TOLD ME, my mama done told me, clicked clank, clicked, clank. From Natchez to Mobile..." I love that song. Who loves us, or wants the very best for us. OUR MOTHERS!

They say when someone is near death; they start calling out for their Mothers. You know death will be soon! Oh the love of a MOTHER! If we could bottle it, we would all be rich. My mother was the most beautiful, sweet, fun person I have ever met. When she walked in, the whole room lit up. If you were at a dinner party, she was the one you wanted to be seated next to, you would definitely have a good time and be entertained.

Three outstanding Junior League ladies were being interviewed by the newspaper and were asked "what woman did they most admire." One said Eleanor Roosevelt, one said Mother Teresa, my sister, Wendy said, our Mother, ELLA MAE KING. We loved that our mother was right up there with the best!

***

My friend BUNZY BRYANT says, "What I hate most about my past is the length of it!"

BARBARA CATTAR lives the life of being so kind, so loving, and giving to all. I was fortunate to be at one of her grandchildren's birthday celebration and heard this! Barbara said when her children were small, singing happy birthday, she would sing, bless you, bless you and it evolved to this, a classic hit! I will never sing HAPPY BIRTHDAY again without the GOOD LORD!...HAPPY BIRTHDAY TO YOU, HAPPY BIRTHDAY TO YOU, HAPPY BIRTHDAY DEAR BARBARA, HAPPY BIRTHDAY TO YOU! Then, the same tune....MAY THE GOOD LORD BLESS YOU, MAY THE GOOD LORD BLESS YOU, MAY THE GOOD LORD BLESS BARBARA, MAY THE GOOD LORD BLESS YOU!

Mike Cage is a strong advocate of taking vitamin supplements. The scientific evidence is so strong and dramatic, it seems reckless not to. Through eating fruits, vegetables, meats and fish taking supplements of vitamins and minerals, we can cut down on the risk of cancer, heart disease and drastically cut down on the aging process. You are not going to be immortal but you have a chance to live in good health to the end of your life and you may live longer. Read everything you can, ask questions, talk to people and experiment with VITAMINS! Watching the news, we heard that taking at least 400 IU, International units, of vitamins and 500 mg of C, helps prevent ALZHEIMERS. Recommended vitamins, also, Selenium and Beta Carotene.

Some research shows that antioxidant vitamins can decrease the heart-disease and cancer risk posed by a fatty diet. Studies show when high doses of vitamins C and E were added to the high fat meal it was as if they had eaten a low fat bowl of Cheerios. There is more and more information that documents the beneficial effect of antioxidants, such as, vitamins work by soaking up dangerous by-products that form when the body metabolizes oxygen. Those by-products, known as free radicals, can damage cells. They are thought to interact with some fats in a way that makes then clog arteries and can produce cellular damage that may lead to cancer. Interesting! Remember; don't think you can eat any thing you want just because you take vitamins. Always remember, everything in MODERATION!

We take most of our vitamins at night and a few in the morning. I never took vitamins until I met Mike Cage. I have been taking them for these last 15 years, if I did not take them, I think I would feel, maybe like riding around without a seat belt on. A scary thought!

***

Mike Cage is a strong believer in looking at your FAMILY HISTORY! He says it is like looking into your future! He inherited the bad cholesterol gene from his Mother, Virginia Ziegler Cage, who died at a very young age. There were 4 sisters in the Ziegler family, Mike's Mother and another sis-

ter died in their 60s', they had the bad gene. The other two sisters, Florence and Norine had the good gene and lived way up into their 90's.

There are wonderful drugs out there to treat these things we inherit. Remember, you have to help yourself too! GOOD DIET, MODERATION. AND EXERCISE!

***

REAL WAYS TO LOOSE WEIGHT

During the holidays they say we can gain 8 to 15 pounds, think about that! We all want to loose 5 or 10 pounds, add another 10 pounds and we have got a problem, no FUN!

Most people burn 1800 to 2000 calories per day. With the holidays it's easy to eat 10,000 calories a day = 2 pounds a day! 8 to 15 pounds is believable! 3500 calories = 1 pound.

We have got to watch what we eat. Count calories! Don't deprive yourself, just watch it!

EXERCISE, EXERCISE, EXERCISE!! EVERYTHING IN MODERATION!!!

INTERESTING! When walking you burn 8 to 10 calories per minute so if you walk 1 hour you burn approximately 480 calories. That is one piece of pie. Not fair. If you walk one hour, say 3 times a week, Makes you think twice about that pie or candy bar.

1 grams of fat=9 calories
1 grams of protein=4 calories
1 carbohydrates=4 calories

A glass of wine, beer or mixed drink is the equivalent of 112 calories and 12 grams of fat. Alcohol, although it isn't fat, is metabolized and stored as fat in the body. So count alcohol in your day's intake and try to cut out something else. Drink lots of water. It is filling and calorie free. Don't go to parties hungry. Go meatless once or twice a week.

Whenever you fall off the wagon, get back on at the next meal or as soon as possible. Deprive yourself by eating really light, you will feel better.

LOSE SLOWLY

Research shows that losing weight slowly improves your chances of not seeing that weight comes roaring back.

LOW FAT IS NOT THE ANSWER

Nothing is making us fatter than low fat/no fat! 1 calorie of fat is no worse than 1 calorie of protein or carbohydrate. Just because it is low fat, we think we can eat more food than we otherwise would.

REDUCE SUGAR. PUMP FIBER INTO YOUR DIET.

It fills you up and speeds food through your body, cutting calorie consumption.

PORTION CONTROL IS VITAL.

Let appetite dictate consumption, not package sizes, restaurant portions or what others eat.

CALORIES ARE ALL THAT COUNT.

Don't obsess over each one, but eat only small portions of high calorie stuff.

CUT OUT LITTLE THINGS.

Instead of drinking juice, drink water instead or maybe try diluting the juice.

EXERCISE.

There is clear connection between regular vigorous exercise, losing weight and keeping it off.

THERE IS NO MAGIC WEIGHT LOSS!

Mike and I really are into the SUGAR BUSTERS, ATKINS, and SOUTH BEACH DIETS! They are an easy way to loose weight and maintain it. As we all know, definite NO NO'S are ALCOHOL, SWEETS, and PASTA. RICE, POTATOES, CORN, BREAD, BEETS, AND CARROTS. AND NOTHING FRIED. They are the things that convert to sugar and are STORED as FAT in the body. The good news is you can have FISH, SHRIMP, STEAK, CHICKEN, SALADS, EGGS, BACON, SAUSAGE, CHEESE, SPINACH, BROCCOLI and a LITTLE RED WINE.

When you get to your desired weight you can always treat yourself to that CHEESEBURGER, chocolate cake or a good ice cold BEER.

***

ANN LANDERS, TIPS FOR A HAPPIER LIFE

Give people more than they expect and do so cheerfully. Don't believe all you hear, spend all you have or sleep all you like. When you say "I'm sorry," look the person in the eye. Love deeply and passionately. You might get hurt, but it is the only way to live life completely. When someone asks you a question you don't want to answer, smile and ask, "Why do you want to know?" When you realize you have made a mistake, take immediate steps to correct it. Smile when you pick up the phone, the caller can hear it in your voice. Live an honorable life, when you get older, you will be glad you did. Remember that not getting what you want may be the best thing that never happens to you. Never interrupt when you are being flattered. Mind your business. Trust in GOD, but lock your car. Marry someone you love to talk to. The older you get, conversation will be one of the principal elements of your relationship.

Speed Lamkin, an old friend of mine, said "LOVE is like JUICY FRUIT GUM!" Speed is one of Monroe's celebrities. He lived in New York, wrote several books, had a play on Broadway for a short time and was a fabulous decorator. Elsa Maxwell,

who was famous for entertaining, was one of Speed's biggest friends. He learned well, because he had some of the best parties around. Not to be missed is Rizzoli's reprinting of one of the greatest social and entertaining guides ever written, "How to Do It or The Lively Art of Entertaining", by the late, great international hostess, ELSA MAXWELL!

***

In the front of all your special cookbooks, write the page number and name of the favorite recipe in that particular book. Sure saves a lot of time!

***

The JOY that you give to others is the JOY that comes back to you. The more you spend in blessing the poor and lonely and sad, the more of your heart's possessing returns to make you glad.   *~John Greenleaf Whittier.*

Mr. TOM SCOTT, of Scott Truck and Tractor, was one of the kindest, most generous men, that ever came out of North Louisiana. He and his family gave and gave and gave, he would say, "you can not outgive GOD! Mr. Scott died in his sleep at age 91. The day before, he had gone to work, to the grocery store and mowed his yard that afternoon. God blessed this wonderful man.

***

This is a prayer written by Albert Schweitzer who was a rare man, a gentle soul and a genius...

A PRAYER FOR OUR ANIMALS

Hear our humble prayer, O God, for our friends, the animals. Especially; for the animals who are suffering; for any that are hunted or lost or deserted or frightened or hungry; for all that must be put to death. We entreat for them all thy mercy and pity, and for those who deal with them, we ask a heart of compassion and gentle hands and kindly words. Make us, ourselves, to be true friends to animals and so to share the blessings of the merciful.

BONE APPETITE TREATS FOR YOUR DOG:
Boo Bancroft's favorite!

4   cups whole wheat
     flour
¾   cup vegetable oil, can
     use canola
2   eggs beaten
1¼ cups shredded cheese
1¼ cups milk

Combine flour and garlic powder in a large bowl. Gradually stir in vegetable oil, beaten eggs and milk. Blend well. Roll out dough to desired thickness. Use bone-shaped cookie cutter to cut treats out. Place on a lightly greased cookie sheet. Bake 25 minutes at 400 degrees. Cool before storing. Cooking time may vary according to thickness of treats.

When baking for your dog, always be sure to check all ingredients to insure that onions are not present. Onions and chocolate can be very toxic to dogs.

My friend KAYDELL JACKSON, of Cody Wyoming, shared this successful diet she used for her grandson, her son Tommy's 150 pound Labrador retriever, CLOVIS, who now lives with she and her better half, Jack Tom. The vet told her the dog was morbidly over weight. They heard about the GREEN BEAN DIET just for DOGS. You substitute half of the food with green beans, say you feed the dog 2 cans of dog food, use I can of dog food and 1 can of green beans. Clovis has lost 25 pounds and loves green beans. He'd rather have the green beans than the dog food!

My children's Grandmother, Marie Louise Snellings, always had 5 or 6 old dogs around. She would boil big pots of chicken backs, necks and rice. It always smelled so good and looked wonderful. I never did, but I always wanted a bite.

SILVER

To clean silver, line the kitchen sink with several sheets of aluminum foil. Sprinkle 1 cup of Tide washing powder and fill sink half-way with hot water and submerge silver. You will not believe how beautiful it is and it only takes seconds. Having a lot of old silver that I use all of the time, I have been to several silver maintenance workshops. They all say use only silver polish and elbow grease. This works and I cannot see any harm to my silver. Sure is quick and easy!

NO KIDDING;

Thomas Edison never learned to spell.
Beethoven could not do simple math.
George Patton was not a good reader.
William the Conqueror could not read any language.

CHRISTMAS gift suggestions from Oren Arnold;
To your enemy, forgiveness.
To your opponent, tolerance.
To a friend, your heart.
To a customer, service.
To all, charity.
To every child, a good example.
To yourself, respect.

JINGLE BELLS

The words and music were written in 1857 by James Pierpont for a Thanksgiving program at his church in Boston. It was so well received that the children were asked to repeat it at Christmas. It has been a Christmas song ever since.

DECK THE HALLS

The music is an old Welsh melody. Mozart used it in a piano and violin duet in the 1700s. The words are believed to be American from the 19th century.

O LITTLE TOWN OF BETHLEHEM

Bishop Phillips Brooks (1835-1903) wrote the words in Philadelphia in 1868. He was recalling his trip to the Holy Land three years earlier, especially the view of Bethlehem from the hills at night. His church organist, Lewis Redner wrote the music for the children's choir.

HARK! THE HERALD ANGELS SING!

The music is from the second chorus of a cantata by Felix Mendelssohn written in 1840 to commemorate Johan Gutenberg and the invention of moveable type. The words are from a hundred years earlier, written in 1739 by Charles Wesley whose brother, John, founded the Methodist Church. In 1855 Dr. William Cummings put the words and music together.

***

SPECIAL GIFTS FROM NORTH LOUISIANA

1.) ULM & Dr. & Mrs. JAMES COFER.

2.) Squire Creek in Choudrant, the JAMES DAVISON Family.

3.) Panola Pepper Sauce, Lake Providence's own son, BUBBA BROWN.

4.) Pecan Oil, Kinloch Plantation, & TOMMY HATFIELD.

5.) LOUISIANA TECH, DOCTOR DAN RENEAU and the KINDNESS shown to THE TULANE FOOTBALL TEAM who were displaced by KATRINA.

Garden District Books
119 Glenmar Avenue
Monroe, Louisiana 71201
(888) 203-5888
Fax: (318) 323-8216

Please send_____ copy(ies) of

Dianne II, Cook & Tell	@	$20.00 each _____
Postage and handling	@	4.00 each _____
Louisiana residents add 9.95% sales tax	@	2.00 each _____
		TOTAL _____

Name _____

Address _____

City _____ State _____ Zip _____

Please make checks payable to Garden District Books.

Garden District Books
119 Glenmar Avenue
Monroe, Louisiana 71201
(888) 203-5888
Fax: (318) 323-8216

Please send_____ copy(ies) of

Dianne II, Cook & Tell	@	$20.00 each _____
Postage and handling	@	4.00 each _____
Louisiana residents add 9.95% sales tax	@	2.00 each _____
		TOTAL _____

Name _____

Address _____

City _____ State _____ Zip _____

Please make checks payable to Garden District Books.

Garden District Books
119 Glenmar Avenue
Monroe, Louisiana 71201
(888) 203-5888
Fax: (318) 323-8216

Please send_____ copy(ies) of

Dianne II, Cook & Tell	@	$20.00 each _____
Postage and handling	@	4.00 each _____
Louisiana residents add 9.95% sales tax	@	2.00 each _____
		TOTAL _____

Name _____

Address _____

City _____ State _____ Zip _____

Please make checks payable to Garden District Books.